Reading Between the Lines Set Two

Reading Between the Lines Set Two is a sequel to the popular *Reading Between the Lines*. It is a resource book for teachers, teaching assistants, SENCOS and Speech and Language Therapists who need to support the development of inference skills in children aged 8–12. These unique guides offer accessible and easy-to-use material specifically targeted to improve inference, which is a crucial element in understanding spoken and written language.

The book provides 370 engaging texts themed around different areas such as place and occupation, and includes short stories about everyday events, magic and adventure. Each short text is accompanied by guiding questions and is carefully graded to allow students to gradually progress from more simple texts with highlighted clues onto more challenging scenarios which will require higher level inferencing skills.

Containing handy photocopiable material, this guide can be used with whole classes, small groups or individual children. It will be particularly valuable to professionals working with children who have Autism Spectrum Disorders or Speech, Language and Communication Needs, who need particular support with inference as they develop their broader social communication skills.

Catherine Delamain is a retired Speech and Language Therapist with over 40 years' experience working with children with Speech, Language and Communication Needs in clinics, schools, special schools and nurseries. She spent several years in association with a Senior Educational Psychologist lecturing to teachers on how to address the needs of children with Speech, Language and Communication Needs in mainstream and special schools. With Jill Spring, she is the co-author of eight books published by Speechmark.

Jill Spring is a retired Speech and Language Therapist who specialised in child Speech and Language Disorder and Autistic Spectrum Disorder. Since qualifying in 1972 she worked in a variety of paediatric settings including community clinics, assessment centres, opportunity playgroups and mainstream schools. From 1996 to 2014 she worked in specialist language units attached to mainstream schools, spending two years managing one of these units. Before retiring in January 2016 she was responsible for coordinating the Education Commissioned Communication Plan support service for children with complex speech, language and communication difficulties. She also worked as part of the multi-disciplinary team responsible for assessment and diagnosis of Autistic Spectrum Disorders in West Dorset.

Reading Between the Lines Set Two

Inference skills for children aged 8-12

Catherine Delamain and Jill Spring

Routledge
Taylor & Francis Group
LONDON AND NEW YORK

First published 2018
by Routledge
2 Park Square, Milton Park, Abingdon, Oxon OX14 4RN

and by Routledge
711 Third Avenue, New York, NY 10017

Routledge is an imprint of the Taylor & Francis Group, an informa business

© 2018 Catherine Delamain and Jill Spring

The right of Catherine Delamain and Jill Spring to be identified as authors of this work has been asserted by them in accordance with sections 77 and 78 of the Copyright, Designs and Patents Act 1988.

All rights reserved. The purchase of this copyright material confers the right on the purchasing institution to photocopy pages which bear the photocopy icon and copyright line at the bottom of the page. No other parts of this book may be reprinted or reproduced or utilised in any form or by any electronic, mechanical, or other means, now known or hereafter invented, including photocopying and recording, or in any information storage or retrieval system, without permission in writing from the publishers.

Trademark notice: Product or corporate names may be trademarks or registered trademarks, and are used only for identification and explanation without intent to infringe.

British Library Cataloguing-in-Publication Data
A catalogue record for this book is available from the British Library

Library of Congress Cataloging-in-Publication Data
Names: Delamain, Catherine, author. | Spring, Jill, author.
Title: Reading between the lines set two : inference skills for children aged 8–12 / Catherine Delamain and Jill Spring.
Description: Abingdon, Oxon ; New York, NY : Routledge, 2018.
Identifiers: LCCN 2017060356 (print) | LCCN 2018014675 (ebook) | ISBN 9781315098500 (ebook) | ISBN 9781138298644 (pbk) | ISBN 9781315098500 (ebk)
Subjects: LCSH: Reading (Elementary) | Reading—Remedial teaching. | Inference—Study and teaching (Elementary)
Classification: LCC LB1573 (ebook) | LCC LB1573 .D265 2018 (print) | DDC 372.4—dc23
LC record available at https://lccn.loc.gov/2017060356

ISBN: 978-1-138-29864-4 (pbk)
ISBN: 978-1-315-09850-0 (ebk)

Typeset in DIN Pro
by Apex CoVantage, LLC

CONTENTS

Preface	**vi**
Introduction	**1**
How to use this book	2
Part 1	**5**
Object	**7**
Action	**22**
Instrument	**36**
Place	**49**
Occupation	**61**
Categories	**73**
Character	**88**
Emotion	**103**
Cause and effect	**117**
Time/era	**131**
Part 2	**145**
Lucky dip	**147**
Stories	**159**

PREFACE

The ability to draw inference is a vital part of understanding language. It is needed for grasping subtleties, innuendos, humour, emotions, contrasts and comparisons. Inference involves making deductions or coming to conclusions based on the given facts. It also involves world knowledge and reasoning. It could be described or referred to as understanding things that are not made explicit in a text. It is important that children are helped where necessary to acquire this essential skill. Many children in mainstream classes have problems in 'getting the main idea', while children with language and communication needs are particularly likely to find it difficult.

The authors of this book have many years' experience of collaborative working with teachers in a range of educational settings. Increased awareness of social communication difficulties, for example Autistic Spectrum Disorder, requires teachers and teaching assistants to address language comprehension beyond the directly stated information.

This book contains 370 short texts providing practice in drawing inference. It is designed for children in Key Stage 2 up to lower Key Stage 3, who will range in age from eight to 12 years. It can be used with both readers and non-readers. The authors hope it will provide a stimulating and interesting way to help develop language comprehension in its fullest sense.

Reading Between the Lines offers:

- Graded texts covering nine of the main recognized categories of inference
- Clear instructions and hints on use

INTRODUCTION

> Inference is a 'foundational skill' – a prerequisite for higher-order thinking and 21st century skills (Marzano, 2010)*

By the age of about seven most children will be able to derive meaning beyond that which is directly stated in the text, using experience, world knowledge and reasoning skills. However, many children who can decode text competently fail to develop this higher level of language comprehension referred to as inference. This limits their ability to identify the main ideas and to understand motives, consequences, cause and effect. It applies particularly to children with additional learning needs, for example those with Autism Spectrum Disorder, Developmental Language Disorder and associated learning difficulties.

The child who relies solely on direct information in the text will find it increasingly difficult to make sense of more complex text. This is particularly true in the case of fiction where inference is needed to understand depth of meaning, including feelings, mood, atmosphere and tension.

Reading Between the Lines is designed to help teachers, teaching assistants and speech and language therapists to develop inference skills in their students. It provides a range of graded texts, giving children practice in identifying implied information. It is aimed at children in Key Stage 2 and lower Key Stage 3 (ages 8–12). It can be used on a one-to-one basis or in small groups.

---

* Cited in Silver, H. F., Dewing, R. T. and Perini, M. L. (2010), *Inference: Teaching Students to Develop Hypotheses, Evaluate Evidence and Draw Logical Conclusions*, Alexandria, VA: ASCD.

How to use this book

Reading Between the Lines consists of a collection of short practice texts. At the end of each text, the child is asked key questions. The answers can be inferred from the text but are not directly stated. Nine main areas of inference are covered. The material in Part 1 of the book contains texts referring to object, action, instrument, place, occupation, category, character, emotion, cause and effect, time and era. The material in Part 2 contains mixed question types and short stories.

The texts in each category in Part 1 are roughly graded in Levels 1 – 4. Levels 1 and 2 provide highlighted 'clues', while in Levels 3 and 4 the clues are not highlighted. There is an introductory activity in each category, which consists of a very brief text and answers.

The levels are not strictly age related, but follow a broadly developmental sequence, in accordance with Dr Marion Blank's work on children's levels of questioning.[†] Younger children will not be expected to reach the higher levels. The target for any child is to be able to deal successfully with the texts he is likely to encounter in the classroom.

Complicating factors include poor short-term auditory memory and poor language processing.

Poor short-term auditory memory refers to difficulty in retaining key facts in spoken information.

Poor language processing refers to difficulty making sense of spoken or written information. The greater quantity of information, the harder this will be.

Support strategies include:

- Work in a distraction-free environment
- Check child understands unfamiliar vocabulary
- Chunk information into no more than two or three sentences at a time. Check child has understood as you go along

---

[†] Blank, M., Rose, S. A. and Berlin, L. J. (1978), *The Language of Learning: The Preschool Years*, New York: Grune & Stratton.

How to use this book

- Go through whole passage a second time
- Back up if possible with visual support

How to start

Select the introductory text from any category in Part 1. Read the text to the child or let the child read it if he/she is able.

After the child has read or listened to the 'story', ask the key question at the end. In some cases, there is more than one question and they should be asked in the order given. If a child is unable to understand the inference at this beginning level, the 'story' can still be used to prompt direct questions whose answer is obvious from the text. This is a first step towards drawing inference. Some older students may be able to go to higher levels and categories in the second half of the book straightaway.

You may want to concentrate on certain categories of inference where the child has had particular difficulty or to work across several categories concurrently.

Non-readers will need the texts to be read to them and the majority of younger students will need some help with reading. Older children may have competent reading skills, but still have little ability to draw inference from what they read. These students can either read to themselves before being asked the key question or be asked to read the texts out loud to the adult.

Teaching at Levels 1 and 2

Introduce the student to the category theme you have chosen, for instance 'These stories are about WHERE something happens' or 'These are about WHEN something happens'.

The first Level 1 text in every category shows the 'clues' printed in bold and a series of questions and prompts are suggested. These provide a guide to working with the ensuing texts. If you are reading to the child, he can still help to identify the clues in bold by pointing to them and you can repeat them to him. *Be sure always to ask the final question 'How do you know?'* This not only clarifies where the child's ideas have been confused or inaccurate, but gives him practice in explaining. Children who get the right answer before the end of the texts are probably able to tackle the next level.

How to use this book

Supplementary questions

If a child cannot answer the key question, don't forget you can ask other questions – refer to the example questions in the first Level 1 texts.

Teaching at Levels 3 and 4

At these levels the 'clues' are not highlighted. You will need to tell the student that they have to read the text or listen to the story and then to identify the 'clues' themselves. Ask the child the target question. If he has read the text to himself, encourage him to use a highlighter to find any 'clues'.

Part 1

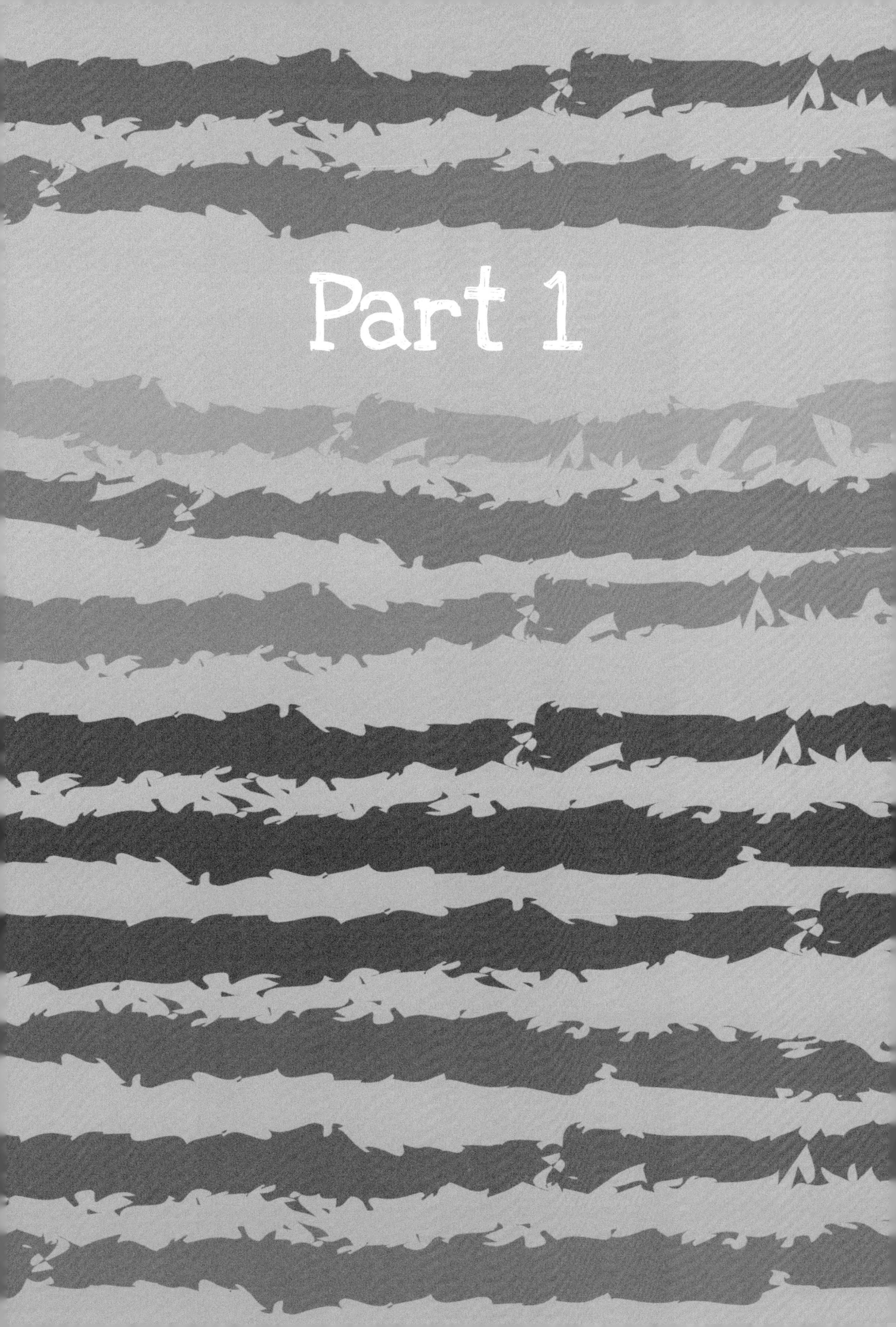

Object

Level 1   8

Level 2   12

Level 3   15

Level 4   17

Reading Between the Lines Set Two

Level 1

Spot the clues that tell you WHAT'S BEING TALKED ABOUT.

Clues might be about:

- What the thing looks like – big/little, shiny, what colour
- What it is made of/what different parts it has
- What you can use it for/what it can do

It might be a person, a creature, a machine, any other kind of 'thing'.

Here is an example. The clues are in bold type.

Sam **went up the path** between the tall trees. He rounded a corner and stared in wonder at what stood in front of him. He could hardly count the **windows**, there were so many. The **chimneys** seemed to reach almost to the sky and there was a funny metal thing **on the roof**, shaped like a fox. It swung round in the wind and Dad said it was a weather vane and it could tell you which way the wind was blowing. A long **flight of steps** led up to a huge **front door**, where a brass knocker shone brightly in the sun. Sam thought this place was big enough for **a giant to live in**.

What was Sam looking at? How do you know? What clues tell you so?

- *Sam was walking up a path towards something*
- *The thing has windows*
- *It has chimneys*
- *It has a roof*
- *There are steps up to a front door*
- *A giant could live in it*

   = It must have been a house

Part 1 – Object

Story 1

Joe couldn't wait to show off his best birthday present to his friends. He decided not to try to show it in the bus, but waited until they were in school. When everybody else had hung up their jackets in the cloakroom, Joe went in to hang up his own. The he slipped quietly into the classroom, and shouted in his loudest voice 'Hey everybody! Look at this!' He flung his arms wide and puffed out his **chest as much as he could to** give everyone a chance to have a good look. It was **bright red**, with the big **yellow-on-white cross in the middle** of the front, and the **Man U logo** in the top left corner. The **sleeves** were a bit too long for Joe, but he had **turned the cuffs back** so it didn't matter. Everyone thought it was great, especially the Man U supporters.

What was Joe wearing? How do you know? What clues tell you so?

Story 2

McTavish wasn't really allowed in the room when the family were having their meals. Mum and Dad both said it was **hard for him to smell all the yummy food** on people's plates and **not to beg**. But sometimes he managed to **sneak in under the table** and he always sat by Oliver. Oliver liked to feel McTavish's **soft furry head** pressed against his leg and usually managed to slip him a little scrap of something. He would be thanked by **a warm lick** from McTavish's tongue. Oliver thought of McTavish as his best friend and loved **the walks** they shared in the park. **Walking McTavish** was the only one of his jobs he really looked forward to – not like cleaning his shoes or emptying the dishwasher!

What or who is McTavish? How do you know? What clues tell you so?

Reading Between the Lines Set Two

Story 3

Since Grandma had come to live with them, the house was a bit of a squeeze. Sukey had to sleep on a camp bed in Mum and Dad's room and Kitty on the spare bed in the tiny back room. One day the girls were packed off to have a sleepover with friends. When they got home for tea, Dad said he had something to show them. The door of the little room had a smart new notice on it saying 'Sukey's and Kitty's room'. Dad flung the door open with a flourish. 'Da-dah!' he said proudly. Dad had done a great job. The **bottom deck** was made up with Sukey's favourite Star Wars **duvet and pillows**, while **the top deck** had Kitty's, with the flower pattern on. Kitty went straight up **the ladder** to try it out, and arrange her family of **cuddly toys**.

What had Dad built in the little bedroom? How do you know? What clues tell you so?

Story 4

The best thing about the new house was the garden. It was much bigger than the one at the old house and had enough lawn to practise bowling and batting, also two big trees. One wonderful **plaything** was already there. It **hung on long ropes** from the **branch of the bigger tree**, with a smooth **wooden seat**. Jacob tried it out at once. With **a push or two** from Mum to get him going, he was soon **swooping up in the air** till he could **almost touch the branch with his toes** and could **see into the next door garden.** Jacob's little brother Adam was determined to have a go, but Mum said he wouldn't be safe. He didn't know **how to hold on to the ropes** tightly enough. They might have to get him a smaller one like the ones in the nursery playground, with a special seat and safety bars.

What did they find in the new garden? What clues tell you so?

Part 1 - Object

Story 5

Bella was in the middle of her favourite game. The **bedroom light** had been **turned off** and Mum had said goodnight, but Bella **could see** well enough **from the backlighting** and was **playing under the duvet**. She was having a competition with her friend about who could get the highest score on Treasure Trail and she was about to beat her own best so far. One more win and she would be in the lead! She gave a shout of triumph without meaning to and at once heard Mum's footsteps coming up the stairs. Quickly she **turned it off** and pulled the duvet up around her ears. Mum opened the door and looked in. 'I hope you aren't still **playing on that wretched thing**' she said. 'Now go to sleep.'

What was Bella playing on? How you know? What clues tell you so?

Story 6

Sally was looking for something really special for her best **friend's birthday**. There was almost too much to choose from. In the end she settled for something that was **all about friendship**. She chose one with a winter theme, which had a **really pretty box**. The shop assistant let her open it to check that everything was inside. There were **the cords**, **the beads** and **charms** like snowflakes or tiny Christmas trees and snowmen. The **beads** were sparkly silver and white. Sally thought that it was just right for Lucy, as her birthday was in December. She could just imagine Lucy wearing it **round her wrist**.

What is Sally going to give Lucy? How do you know? What clues tell you so?

Reading Between the Lines Set Two

Level 2

Story 1

It was the afternoon of Evie's birthday and she was going to be three. It was **her first real party** and **Mum was decorating the room**. She had a **big box of them to blow up** and was beginning to **wish she had a pump for the job**, instead of blowing them up by mouth. She had done enough for every child to have three, but **every so often one would pop** and she would have to start counting again. She had to make sure there were plenty of pink ones, as that was Evie's favourite colour.

What was Mum decorating the room with? How do you know? What clues tell you so?

Story 2

The one in the playground was the best that Noah and Lewis had ever been on. It was a really big one, with **safety netting round it** so you **couldn't bounce yourself out** and onto the ground. Only two people were allowed on at the same time, which Dad said was a good idea. Both boys **could bounce pretty high** by now and Noah was **trying to turn over in the air** and land on his feet. They longed to have one of their own, but the garden wasn't big enough to fit a proper one in.

What were the boys playing on? What clues tell you so?

Part 1 - Object

Story 3

Millie was thrilled with the present her Uncle Jack had brought with him. Inside the box were **little pots of paint**, **paint brushes** and a **packet of stencils.** The label on the box said 'Garden Set'. The stencils were **of flowers and trees, butterflies and birds**. Millie disappeared with it up to her room and was gone for ages. After an hour had passed, Mum went up to see what was going on. She opened the bedroom door and peered in. Millie had gorgeous glittery **butterflies all down both arms** and was just starting on her tummy.

What present did Uncle Jack bring Millie? How do you know? What clues tell you so?

Story 4

The reception class teacher came in to Mrs Daly's classroom and asked if she could have a word with the children. 'Do any of you have a **pond in your garden**?, 'she asked. 'Or do any of you go near **streams or rivers**? I want to teach the little ones about **how frogs grow**.' She explained what she needed. Harry said he could help. The pond in their garden was **full of the little black wriggly things**. That evening he **fished some out with a shrimping net** and next day took a jarful in to school. The reception children were very excited.

What did Harry take in to school? How do you know? What clues tell you so?

Reading Between the Lines Set Two

Story 5

The **swimming pool** was as busy as usual and echoed with shouts and splashing. Ted's swimming had come on in leaps and bounds and he had just done two widths when he saw his **friend Will coming out of the shower**. Will jumped in beside him. 'Hi', he said. 'I can **stay an hour** and now I don't have to keep swimming down to the shallow end **to see the time**.' He **pointed to his wrist**. '**Backlit numbers** and **waterproof**!', he said proudly, 'Got it with my saved up pocket money.' Ted was very envious. He thought he would put one like that at the top of his present list.

What was Will wearing? How do you know? What clues tell you so?

Story 6

Maya worked her way along the **shelves**. The first lot were marked '**Ages 8–10**'. She went on a bit further. '**Ages '11–13.**' That was more like it. Now to find her favourite **author** and the new one in the series that had **just been published**. Maya **hoped against hope there would be a copy**. Elsa Blackmore was so popular that anything new by her just flew off the shelves. Maya was thrilled to find a single copy. She grabbed it and set off to the pay counter. She could hardly wait to get home and curl up on the settee with it.

What has Maya just bought? What clues tell you so?

Part 1 - Object

Level 3

In the next stories, you have to *find the clues yourself*.

Story 1

Mum was on a diet. She had been really good about it – no cakes, no biscuits, no sweets, only a little bread and lots and lots of fruit and vegetables. She was just coming out of the chemist with Layla when she suddenly stopped. 'I'll just pop over and see how much I've lost', she said. Layla watched Mum stand on the machine, and saw a big smile spread over her face. 'Three pounds in two weeks', Mum said triumphantly as she came back to Layla.

What sort of machine did Mum use in the chemist's? What clues tell you so?

Story 2

Ben was sitting on the edge of the quay. He had a homemade fishing rod made of a bit of string tied to a stick and a hook on the end of the string with a bit of meat on it. Dangling his line into the water, there was a sudden tug. Ben pulled it up. It was his best catch of the day and as he unhooked it he reckoned it was at least four centimetres across its shell. Its claws were enormous. Almost big enough to be worth taking home for supper.

What had Ben caught? How do you know? What clues tell you so?

Reading Between the Lines Set Two

Story 3

It just had to be that one that Jamilla dropped and broke. Grandma's favourite, that she always used when she had friends to tea. It was made of really thin china and had a pretty pattern of roses on it. Grandma kept it on the dresser in a special place. Now there was nothing left but the handle and a lot of tiny broken bits.

What had Jamilla broken? How do you know? What clues tell you so? Could it be more than one thing?

Story 4

The family were off to the beach. The picnic was packed and rugs, sun cream, skimmer boards and loads of other things had been stowed into the car. 'Everything else you need is up to you', Mum said. 'If you have to go stark naked into the sea or stay wet for ages afterwards, it's your responsibility. You've got three minutes to think!'

What two things was Mum reminding the children to take? How do you know? What clues tell you so?

Story 5

For Charlie's birthday treat they were going to their favourite speciality restaurant. 'Did you see the extra-big ones last time we were there?', 'Charlie asked. 'They were the size of cartwheels! There was so much stuff piled on them I lost count. Anchovies and tomatoes and cheese and some things I didn't even know. Could Max and I have one between us to share?'

What sort of restaurant were the family going to? How do you know? What clues tell you so?

Part 1 - Object

Story 6

Dave lifted it reverently out of the box, gloating over the glossy finish of the wood. He plugged it in and gently tried plucking and tapping the strings. Thrilled, he strummed a little tune. This made his old one look like a child's toy. What a birthday present! Now his place in the group was safe.

What has Dave been given for his birthday? How do you know? What clues tell you so?

Level 4

Story 1

It was time for lights out in the bunkhouse, and Callum was feeling homesick. He got the little leather case out and propped it up beside his pillow. Now he could look at his parents whenever he needed to give himself a bit of courage.

What did Callum put beside his pillow? How do you know? What clues tell you so?

Can you explain why he wanted it?

Story 2

Barney from next door was in the garden again. He was no longer the adorable little ball of fluff he had been six months ago. Now he was a hunter and he had his eye on Sukey's bird table. She opened the window and waved her arms at him. 'It'll be a bucket of water next time', she shouted.

Who or what was in Sukey's garden? How do you know? What clues tell you?

What did Sukey mean she might do to him?

Reading Between the Lines Set Two

Story 3

'Eat it quickly', said Nan, 'In this heat, it'll melt in no time.' Jude was already having a struggle. Some of it was running down his arm and he had chocolate all over his face. 'Give it to me', said Nan, 'I'll hold it for you while you lick.'

What was Jude eating? How do you know? What clues tell you so?

Story 4

The door of the surgery kept on opening and every time Tara was sure it was her turn. She could almost feel the prick in her arm already. At long last, the door opened again. This time there was no doubt that the figure with the white coat was looking at her.

Who came in through the door? How do you know? What clues tell you so?

Can you guess what Tara was waiting to have done?

Story 5

Bella woke up with a start. It was the same dream again – the great scaly monster was flying in through her window, breathing fire and smoke as it came. 'Teach me to read adventure books at bedtime', she thought.

What had Bella been dreaming about? How do you know? What clues tell you so?

Part 1 - Object

Story 6

Tom had made a frightful fuss when Nan had given it the final little tweak to pull it out. Now it had pride of place in a glass by Tom's bed and he showed it off to everyone.

He kept feeling the gap with his tongue and checking in the mirror to see that it was really gone.

What was in the glass by Tom's bed? How do you know? What clues tell you so?

Story 7

Rashid climbed into bed and wriggled his way under the covers. He gave a shriek as his toes met something warm and furry. He laughed at his fright when the furry object gave a plaintive 'miau'.

What had Rashid found in his bed? How do you know? What clues tell you so?

Story 8

Emma could hardly believe that the little black seed she had planted back in the spring could have turned into something taller than her, its great round yellow head turning towards the sun.

What was Emma looking at? How do you know? What clues tell you so?

Reading Between the Lines Set Two

Story 9

There was a thud against the window and something fell to the ground. When Katie ran outside, she found the little body lying perfectly still. Its eyes were closed. She stroked the lovely blue and yellow feathers and decided to give it a proper burial under the apple tree.

What caused the thud on the window? How do you know? What clues tell you so?

Can you explain why this might have happened?

Story 10

Mum was muttering to herself the way she always did when she had lost something. 'I had the darn thing half an hour ago when I was making the list for the supermarket and when I got that number I wanted. What on earth can I have done with it?'

What has Mum lost? How do you know? What clues tell you so?

Could there be more than one right answer?

Story 11

Ted was really at a disadvantage these days when they went cross-country and envied his friend Jack's 18 speed gears and off road tyres.

What did Ted want? How do you know? What clues tell you so?

Part 1 - Object

Story 12

'How's the lawn coming on?', called Grandma from the kitchen window. Grandpa was sitting in the sun with a newspaper on his knee. 'The machine's broken down and the mechanic can't get here till tomorrow', he said, smiling cheerfully. 'And it says in the paper rain is forecast for tomorrow.'

What machine has broken down? What clues tell you so?

**Do you think Grandpa enjoys the job he has been doing?
Does he hope to be able to do it tomorrow?**

Action

Level 1	23
Level 2	27
Level 3	30
Level 4	32

Part 1 - Action

Level 1

Spot the clues that tell you *WHAT'S GOING ON*.

Clues might be about:

- What people are doing or going to do – jumping, climbing, running a race
- What animals or other creatures are doing
- What's happening, is going to happen, has happened

Here is an example. The clues are in bold type.

Mandy had been there for ages, but at last she had **nearly made a choice**. She took the ones she liked best and found the **assistant.** In the changing room, Mandy **took her skirt off** and **hung it on a peg**. Then she **took the blue pair** off the hanger and **put one leg in.** It was a bit of a battle to **get the other leg in** and even more of a struggle to get them over her tummy. When she **tried to do up the zip,** it was hopeless. Mandy looked at herself in the mirror. Oh dear, she was **bulging out all over**. She struggled again to get out of the things. She went back to the assistant. 'I'm afraid I need about two sizes bigger', she said sadly.

What was Mandy doing? How do you know? What clues tell you so?

- *She was choosing things*
- *She found an assistant*
- *She must have been in a shop*
- *She took her skirt off*
- *She put one leg in and then the other leg*
- *When she had pulled them up, she couldn't do the zip up*

  = *She must have been trying to buy some jeans or trousers*

Reading Between the Lines Set Two

Story 1

Jacob's little brother had just had his fourth birthday and he was very excited about **his best present**. He was **sitting on it** now, clutching the **handlebars** tightly. Dad was keeping hold of the **saddle**. 'Right', Dad said. 'Off we go.' Noah began to **pedal**, slowly at first and then faster and started to **move across the grass** with Dad running beside him. After a bit Dad let go and Noah was on his own, balanced by the **stabilizers**. All of a sudden, he realized that he was doing it by himself and, of course, he fell off in a heap. '**I can ride**, I can ride Dad', he shouted. 'Let's do it again.'

What was Noah doing? How do you know? What clues tell you so?

Story 2

Robin and his friend Jared had **gone to the wood** to have their favourite competition. It was about **who could get the highest** in two minutes. Robin usually won, but Jared was pretty good, too. Jared found a perfect beech with **branches spaced just right**. The only problem was **getting to the first branch**, which was just out of his reach. 'You'll have to **give me a leg up**', he said. Robin agreed, but said he should be allowed extra time to make up. Once he was on the first branch, Jared **went up easily**, sending down **a shower of twigs and leaves** behind him. Then Robin called 'Time's up! Come on down. My turn now.'

What were the boys doing for their competition? How do you know? What clues tell you so?

Part 1 - Action

Story 3

Jamilla had a **plaster on her right leg**. She had broken the leg really badly and **for a week** had to **stay in a wheelchair** and **be pushed everywhere**. She **was fed up** with it and had made up her mind she was **going to get about somehow by herself**. She tried standing up, but the weight of the plaster made her lose her balance and she grabbed for the chair. Then she had another go and this time it was better. The third time, **Jamilla held the bad leg up off the ground** and, **on her good leg**, **like a rabbit or a kangaroo**, she **made it across the room**. She was really pleased with herself; now at least she could be independent in the house.

How did Jamilla get across the room? How do you know? What clues tell you so?

Story 4

Lucy and her Mum were out for a **walk with Fudge**. The first bit of the walk was on the road, but soon they came to their favourite pathway into the fields. It was a **popular place fo**r the **local pet owners**. They had just **let Fudge off his lead** when they saw **Lucy's friend** Kitty **haring across the field shouting 'Nutmeg! Nutmeg**!'. Kitty came to a halt in front of them, panting and out of breath. 'Did you see him?', she asked. 'I'll be in such **trouble if I lose him**. He was **chasing a cat**.' And she set off again as fast as she could, still **calling Nutmeg's name** and **blowing her whistle**.

What was Kitty doing? How do you know? What clues tell you so?

Copyright material from Catherine Delamain & Jill Spring (2018),
Reading Between the Lines Set Two, Routledge

Reading Between the Lines Set Two

Story 5

Grandpa and Grandma had just moved house. Grandma hated the **walls of the new house looking so bare**, so now **Grandpa was up a ladder**, with **a hammer in his hand**, a **tape measure** in his pocket and a **pencil for making marks on the wall**. It was Will's job to hand things up when Grandpa asked for them. Grandpa was **measuring** where to put Grandma's favourite, **the one with the bowl of red poppies**. 'Right', said Grandpa. **'Hook please.'** Will passed one up. Three **quick taps** and it was **firmly in**. 'Now Grandma's poppies', said Grandpa. Will passed it up. 'I think we'll do that **little one with the horses** next', Grandpa said. 'It should **just fit over the bookcase**.'

What was Grandad doing? How do you know? What clues tell you so?

Story 6

Some friends had come to help and the living room was getting a bit crowded! Someone was balancing on a chair to **hang up the balloons**. Mum was putting **little bags of presents** into a box in the corner, ready to **give out to the children** at the end of the party. A lady was arranging **sandwiches** on the table and someone he had never seen before was sticking **candles** into the **big chocolate cake**. 'Hope she knows how many to put in', thought Kasim to himself. As there didn't seem to be anything he could do to help, he thought he might as well go and get himself ready. He was going to wear his new Chelsea T-shirt to celebrate having **reached the great age of eight**.

What were the people in the living room doing? How do you know? What clues tell you so?

What anniversary do you think they were celebrating?

Part 1 - Action

Level 2

Story 1

They had picnicked **on the sand** and it was getting **really hot**. It was time to **cool down**. The children took off their sunhats but kept on their sandals, as Mum said they would **be OK in the water** and would make walking over the stones a bit easier. Dad put on Millie's armbands for her. Then the three of them set off, picking their way **over the pebbles and some slippery rocks**, to where **the little waves were sparkling** invitingly in the sunshine. Mum followed behind, carrying an armful of towels.

What were the children going to do? How do you know? What clues tell you so?

Story 2

Grace was next in the queue. The girl in front **had been done with a wonderful cat's face** and black whiskers. The lady asked Grace what she would like to be. Grace **chose a butterfly** and sat down in the chair under the light. The lady **started with Grace's cheeks** and worked her way a bit at a time **all over her face**. It took about five minutes and Grace was starting to feel bored when the lady said 'There you are!'. She **handed Grace a mirror** and Grace **saw a gorgeous butterfly** with brightly coloured wings looking back at her.

What was the lady doing to Grace? How do you know? What clues tell you so?

Reading Between the Lines Set Two

Story 3

The family had looked at the cages where the tropical birds were and seen monkeys, penguins and zebras. Next on the list was Liam's favourite place. They went down some steps and along a corridor and finally reached the first of the **huge tanks.** It was softly lit, and filled with rocks, stones and sand and **seaweed waving in the water**. At first, it seemed as if there was nothing else in there. Just as he was about to give up, **an enormous shape** swam out from behind a rock and came straight towards Liam, its **jaws open to show the rows of sharp teeth**. They were almost nose to nose!

What was Liam doing? How do you know? What clues tell you so?

What did he see?

Story 4

'You can do this at home easily', Mrs Wood the teacher said. She showed them how to **soak a bit of material and put it in a shallow dish. Then she opened the packet** and shook the **tiny black specks** into her hand. She sprinkled them onto the wet material and placed the dish on a sunny windowsill. '**They will start to sprout** in just a day or two. In a week you should be able to snip some off and put it in your sandwiches.'

What was Mrs Wood doing? How do you know? What clues tell you so?

Part 1 - Action

Story 5

The crowd hushed as the two men took **climbed up into the opposite corners**. The bell clanged and the two moved fast towards each other, **fists up**, dancing on their toes like ballerinas and weaving from side to side. There was **a flurry of fists** and the challenger fell back, shaking his head. For a few minutes it was evenly balanced and the referee had no need to intervene, but then slowly the champion was being **forced backwards towards the ropes**.

What were the two men doing? How do you know? What clues tell you so?

Story 6

It was hot **in the car**, even with the air conditioning on. They tried having the windows open instead, but that was worse. The **line of cars in front of them** seemed to stretch out for ever and they had **hardly moved for the last five minutes**. **Dad** was getting worried and **kept looking at his watch**. Mum had dished out packets of crisps and bottles of water, but those weren't going to last much longer. 'It's going to be a **close run thing at the airport**, at this rate', Dad said.

What was happening? How do you know? What clues tell you so?

Why do you think Dad was worried?

Copyright material from Catherine Delamain & Jill Spring (2018), *Reading Between the Lines Set Two*, Routledge

Reading Between the Lines Set Two

Level 3

In the next stories, you have to *find the clues yourself*.

Story 1

As they drove along the road, Uncle Ahmed was commenting – as he always did – on how the trees were looking, whether they seemed healthy and whether they needed cutting back. Uncle Ahmed was a tree surgeon and trees were his passion. One great oak they passed had a branch that hung right over the road, almost making the road into a tunnel. 'Better let the Council know about that one when we get home', Uncle Ahmed said. 'Can't think why they've let it go for so long.'

**What did Uncle Ahmed think might happen? How do you know?
What clues tell you so?**

Story 2

Tom watched as the man put on his flippers and adjusted his mask. Then he hoisted the cylinder on to his back and put the breathing tube into his mouth. He balanced carefully on the side of the rubber dinghy, and gave his partner the 'OK' sign, thumb and forefinger together making an 'O'. When he tipped himself backwards, there was hardly a splash, just a trail of bubbles to show where he had been. The other man looked at his watch and settled down to wait.

**What do you think the two men are doing? How do you know?
What clues tell you so?**

What do you think the first man might be hoping to see?

Part 1 - Action

Story 3

Lewis looked at his watch. They had already been waiting for 20 minutes and there were still lots of people in front of them. 'The programme begins at 5.30 and it's 5.15 now', he said to Bella. 'Shall we go on waiting? We'll only miss the trailers and the cartoons; the main feature doesn't start till 5.45.' 'Fine by me', Bella said. 'Shall I go and get the popcorn while you keep our place here?'

What were Lewis and Bella doing? How do you know? What clues tell you so?

Story 4

Geoff Summers was in first. He placed his bat firmly in the crease and squared it up. He looked down the pitch to where Rutherford, the opposing team's star bowler, was rubbing the ball on his trousers and walking towards the start of his run. Summers took a deep breath, glanced towards the stands where his family were watching and prepared to do his best.

What was Geoff Summers doing? How do you know? What clues tell you so?

Story 5

Layla stood at the top, looking at the switchback course in front of her. Other children were swooping up and down, making it look easy. Layla had never done more than fairly gentle slopes before, but she was determined to tackle this one. After all the wheedling it had taken to get here, she couldn't back out now. She put her board down and took a deep breath.

What was Layla going to do? How do you know? What clues tell you so?

Reading Between the Lines Set Two

Story 6

The car was off the road, on the grass verge. Clouds of steam were rising from under the bonnet. A lady and two children were sitting on the bank, passing a bottle of water between them. Leaning against the car, a man was talking on his mobile. 'What bad luck', said Mum as they drove past. 'If they were heading for our ferry they haven't a chance of making it.'

What had happened to the people at the side of the road? How do you know? What clues tell you so?

Can you guess where Mum and the family were going?

Level 4

Story 1

Nicky stood up holding on to the railings and tried to get her balance. Then she managed two slides forward before falling again. The chill from the ice was beginning to reach her toes and fingers, but she was determined to persevere.

What was Nicky doing? How do you know? What clues tell you so?

Story 2

Aisha felt close to tears as she passed the flats where her Gran used to live. The funeral was a year ago now, but it still felt like yesterday.

What had happened in Aisha's family? How do you know? What clues tell you so?

Part 1 - Action

Story 3

Grandma was washing the floor in her spotless kitchen. 'Anyone going in there in the next half hour is on my black list', she said.

What did Grandma think would happen if the children went into the kitchen? Would Grandma mind? What makes you think so? What clues tell you so?

Story 4

Adam knew he was already in trouble, as it was five past nine. 'Might as well make a day of it', he thought. 'I've got 100% for attendance so far this term.' At that moment, he spotted Mr Frost across the street and dived into the nearest shop until the history teacher was out of sight.

What is Adam planning to do? How do you know? What clues tell you so?

Has he ever done this before?

Story 5

Kai had a new book on his Kindle called *Witches, Wizards, and Scary Happenings*. He had the house to himself and was looking forward to reading it, but first he made sure the front door was locked. He even looked under the beds and in the hall cupboard. He felt a bit of a fool, but that didn't stop him.

What did Kai half believe might happen while he was reading his book? How do you know? What clues tell you so?

Can you explain why he felt a bit of a fool while he was locking the door and looking under the beds?

Reading Between the Lines Set Two

Story 6

Alice watched as her aunt stretched the clingfilm over the top of the last jar, wrote 'Strawberry' on the label and put it with the others and the honey and peanut butter, on the shelf. 'That should last us for a good long time', she said. 'Do you want to scrape the bowl out before I wash it up? There's enough to put on one piece of bread.'

What has Alice's aunt been doing? How do you know? What clues tell you so?

Story 7

Dad straightened up from rinsing the wheel hubs and gave a final rub to the number plate. He coiled up the hose and emptied out the bucket of soapy water. 'Looks more like a new model now than a six-year old one', he said to Jo in a satisfied voice.

What has Dad been doing? How do you know? What clues tell you so?

Story 8

This was always Grandad's big moment. He disappeared and half an hour later into the living room came Father Christmas, complete with beard and scarlet cloak. The visiting children clustered round excitedly and Father Christmas winked at Sasha as he began to give out the presents.

What had Grandad been doing? How do you know? What clues tell you so?

Has he ever done this before, do you think?

Part 1 - Action

Story 9

The man slowed to a stop, panting and out of breath, as the Number 10 vanished round the corner. He looked back up the road and frantically hailed a cruising taxi.

What had the man been doing to get out of breath? How do you know? What clues tell you so?

Was he in a great hurry? What makes you think so?

Story 10

Ed banged in a final nail and stood back to look at his handiwork. He had designed it to be big enough for both the guinea pigs and easy to move around every day to a fresh patch of grass.

What has Ed been doing? How do you know? What clues tell you so?

Story 11

Nan stood up. 'Phew', she said. 'Last one! I'm glad you don't have four friends for a sleepover all that often. I've run out of sheets!'

What has Nan been doing? How do you know? What clues tell you so?

Story 12

Jude shouted up the stairs to Mum: 'Mrs Baines's milk is still on her doorstep and it's getting really hot out already.' Mum popped the baby into her cot and went round to knock on Mrs Baines's door.

What did Jude and Mum think might have happened next door? How do you know? What clues tell you so?

Can you see why Jude was worried?

Copyright material from Catherine Delamain & Jill Spring (2018), *Reading Between the Lines Set Two*, Routledge

Instrument

Level 1	37
Level 2	40
Level 3	43
Level 4	45

Part 1 - Instrument

Level 1

Spot the clues that tell you WHAT IT IS.

Clues might be about:

- What it looks like
- What you do with it
- What it's used for

Here is an example. The clues are in bold type.

Gran was hunting about along the shelves and on the chairs in the living room. Ellie knew what she was looking for. 'Here you are, Gran', she said. 'Down the side of your chair. Lucky you didn't sit on them, they break so easily.' Gran **perched them on her nose** and peered at Ellie. '**You're still a bit of a blur**', she said. 'These are the wrong ones. I **need the ones for reading the paper** and doing the crossword.' Ellie returned to the hunt, but without success. Eventually she went to ask Mum. 'Try beside her bed', Mum said. 'She **wears them when she reads in bed** last thing at night.' Sure enough, there they were, on the floor in a bedroom slipper. It was a great day when Gran **went to the optician** and came back with a **single new pair**. '**These do for long distance** and **close work**', Gran said. 'And they gave me this neat little chain so I can hang them round my neck when I don't need them.'

What had Gran lost? How do you know? What clues tell you so?

- *She perched them on her nose*
- *She still couldn't see Ellie very well, she was a bit of a blur*
- *She needed the ones for reading the paper*
- *They were the same ones that she wore to read in bed at night*
- *Gran went to the optician*
- *She got some new ones that worked for long distance and close work*

   = She must have been talking about glasses (spectacles)

Reading Between the Lines Set Two

Story 1

The wind had been blowing hard all night and in the morning the **street and the doorstep were covered with leaves**. Mum was fussy about the front step; she reckoned if the leaves got wet people would slip over on them. 'Be a dear and **clear them up for me**', she said to Jamie. 'You can put them in the garden waste bin.' Jamie quite **enjoyed sweeping the steps and the pavement** and the next-door neighbour looked over the fence to admire his work. 'I'll pay you to do mine for me', he said.

What did Jamie use to clear up the steps and the pavement? How do you know? What clues tell you so?

Story 2

Auntie **took another of Uncle Bill's shirts** off the pile. '**Why** on earth **your uncle can't wear wrinkle-free ones** like you boys do, I'll never know', she said crossly, as she **spread the crumpled blue shirt out on the board**. '**This job takes me a couple of hours every week** and he only wears the things once before he chucks them in the washing basket again.' Josh had to admit that Uncle Bill's **shirts did look very crisp and smart** when Auntie had finished with them.

What was Auntie using to make the shirts look crisp and smart? How do you know? What clues tell you so?

Story 3

Lucy's ball had fallen into thick bushes, but Lucy, as usual, was determined to get it out without help. She pushed her way in and emerged triumphantly with the ball, but also with **a bleeding finger**. 'It's only a tiny scratch', she said to her Mum, 'but **it won't stop bleeding. Can you put something on it?**' 'You know what we always use', Mum said. 'Fetch me the **box of waterproof ones from the bathroom cabinet.**' Lucy soon had a neat dressing on her finger.

What did her Mum put on Lucy's finger? How do you know? What clues tell you so?

What sort of girl does this story show Lucy to be, do you think?

Part 1 - Instrument

Story 4

Year 6 had a really good band and Mrs Turner the music teacher had agreed to work with the players for the end-of-year concert. She **played as well as conducting** and the group were looking forward to this evening's rehearsal. They all arrived early and waited eagerly for Mrs Turner to come. Right on time **she arrived**, **sat down** and **arranged the music in front of her**. 'You might like to listen to this piece before we start', she said. 'Watch my fingers. It **uses almost only the black notes,** which is rather fun.'

What instrument does Mrs. Turner play? How do you know? What clues tell you so?

Story 5

Maisie was making **big posters** to stick up on the school board, to invite people to the disco. She had **typed it out carefully** and included lots of different fonts and colours. She was rather pleased with it. She **fed a stack of paper into the machine** and **pressed the start button for one copy**. The first one rolled out and Maisie grabbed it. It looked absolutely great. She pressed '20' and 'start' and the rest of **the copies began to roll out**.

What was Maisie using to produce the posters? How do you know?
What clues tell you so?

Story 6

Ty and Aidan had gone into the barn to try to find Aidan's old go-kart. The **thin beam of light** that Aidan was directing into the dark corners was not much good, but was better than nothing ... until it went out. 'Bother, the **batteries must have conked out**', said Aidan. Stumbling and groping their way, the boys made it back to the door of the barn. Luckily, there was a bright moon shining outside.

What had the boys been using for a light? How do you know? What clues tell you so?

Copyright material from Catherine Delamain & Jill Spring (2018),
Reading Between the Lines Set Two, Routledge

Level 2

Story 1

Rick was waiting for an interview for the stage school. He was wildly excited and nervous at the same time. Mum looked at him. 'You've got a **smudge on your nose**', she said, licking a corner of her hankie and rubbing at Rick's nose. 'And **you look as if you've been dragged through a hedge backwards**.' She **fished in her handbag**. 'Here, see if you can make your hair lie down properly.'

What did Mum fish out from her handbag? How do you know? What clues tell you so?

Story 2

Marko had a **splinter in his finger** and he did hate **having splinters dug out**. His grandmother was very good at it and **knew just what to use**. She kept her **sewing things** in a big wooden work box with a satin lining. Grandma began to poke gently round the splinter. Apart from a few 'ouches' Marko bore it bravely. Once the splinter was out, Grandma looked for the other thing she always kept in her work box – a bag of toffees.

What did Grandma use to get Marko's splinter out? How do you know? What clues tell you so?

Why did she keep toffees in her workbox, do you think?

Part 1 - Instrument

Story 3

The head gardener and his team were tackling some of the shrubs in the park. They had got very overgrown and now you could hardly see what shape they were meant to be. Rosie and her Gran stopped to watch. One man was starting on a huge bush, first thinning the lower part and gradually working his way up, trimming and clipping. Almost as if by magic, a shape began to emerge. 'I think it's going to be a dog', guessed Rosie. The gardener looked round and laughed. 'Guess again', he said. When he had finished, the shrub had been transformed into a stately peacock.

What was the gardener using to shape the bush? How do you know? What clues tell you so?

Story 4

When it got dark Sophy's Grandpa took the girls into the garden. '**Look up at the sky** and you can see **millions more stars** than you ever see at home', he said. 'There's so much artificial light from houses and cars and street lamps in London that it blots out the starlight.' They went upstairs to where Grandpa's most precious possession stood by a tall window. Grandpa showed them how to **put their eye to the viewfinder** and focus on different groups of stars. They thought the **starry sky** was the most magical thing they had ever seen.

What is Grandpa's most precious possession? How do you know? What clues tell you so?

Reading Between the Lines Set Two

Story 5

It was Alina's **11th birthday** and she knew exactly what was going to be in the beautifully wrapped **parcel** on the kitchen table. Her **old one was pretty basic** and only had a camera and a couple of apps on it. She was absolutely thrilled with the **new one**. It had not only **a camera**, but **loads of apps** including **a diary**. It **even had satnav on it** – not that she really needed it, but it would be fun to be able to help Dad out if they ever got lost! She sat down to transfer all her friends' numbers into it.

What was Alina's birthday present? How do you know? What clues tell you so?

How would she be able to help Dad, do you think?

Story 6

Mum looked at the pile of **clean washing** in the laundry basket and then she looked at the sky. 'Here comes the next downpour', she said. 'I was going to put this lot out on the line, but if you need your football kit by two o'clock it can't wait.' She **stuffed the contents** of the basket **into the machine** and **set the timer** for 40 minutes. Umar looked at his watch. Mum was cutting things a bit fine, but at least he could be organizing his boots and kitbag and snacks. He went off upstairs.

Where did Mum put the washing? How do you know? What clues tell you so?

What was Umar going to do that afternoon, do you think?

Part 1 - Instrument

Level 3

In the next stories, you have to *find the clues yourself*.

Story 1

Aunt Berta was doing her morning housework and she had what she called her 'new toy'. This one ran on batteries, so there were no wires to wrap round the furniture or to trip over. It was really quiet too – her old one was so noisy that it terrified the cat. There were attachments for reaching up to the ceiling, for poking into corners, for doing the stairs and for cleaning the curtains without sucking them into its insides! Celina watched admiringly as Aunt Berta whirled around the room.

What was Aunt Berta's new 'toy'? How do you know? What clues tell you so?

Why does she call it a toy, do you think?

Story 2

The choir was rehearsing for the carol service and Jack was one of three who had been chosen to sing a solo. His turn was next. Chris handed over to him and moved aside. The music started and Jack started to sing, but his voice was so soft it could hardly be heard. 'Hold it up near your mouth', muttered Chris into his ear. Jack went red with embarrassment – he hadn't even switched it on! The next attempt was a lot better.

What had Jack forgotten to use? How do you know? What clues tell you so?

Reading Between the Lines Set Two

Story 3

Dad attached one end to the garden tap and put the other end into Charlie's hand. 'If you turn the nozzle clockwise you get a stronger jet, and anticlockwise you get a gentler spray. Don't aim the strong jet at the flowers, you could damage them', he said, turning on the tap. 'Try and give everything a good soaking.' Charlie twiddled the nozzle and a jet of water shot out. It was Max's bad luck that he came down the steps at that moment.

What was Charlie using? How do you know? What clues tell you so?

What was Max's bad luck, do you think?

Story 4

A gang of men was working among the trees in the Great Park. One giant tree lay felled in a clearing. Myra and Dave could hear the scream of the machine and as they watched the great blade sliced through the trunk as easily as if it were butter. There was already a huge pile of logs heaped on a cart and Myra was thrilled to see that the cart was going to be pulled by two huge shire horses, not a tractor. 'We have to stay and watch', she said.

What were the men using? How do you know? What clues tell you so?

Story 5

Maddelyn was spending Saturday helping out at the stables where she went for riding lessons. Today she had been put in charge of grooming her favourite pony, Grasshopper. She had worked until her arms ached and first she had got all the mud and clumps of hair out. Now she was trying to get Grasshopper's coat as smooth and shiny as she possibly could. She was thinking it was a good thing she didn't have to work so hard on her own hair.

What was Maddelyn using to groom Grasshopper? How do you know? What clues tell you so?

Part 1 - Instrument

Story 6

A mixed group of Year 3s and Year 4s had been given the job of measuring one another and making a chart of everybody's height. It was a tricky job, as you had to get the person you were measuring to stand up straight and keep absolutely still. Rob and Andy had hatched a plan. They worked as a pair, one to hold the top end and the other to stretch it down to the floor and read the numbers off. The people who had tried using a ruler soon gave up and copied Rob and Andy.

What were the boys using to measure people with? How do you know? What clues tell you so?

Can you work out why it would have been difficult to use a ruler?

Level 4

Story 1

The soloist stood up and looked at the conductor, tucked his instrument under his chin and gently drew the bow across the strings.

What instrument was the soloist playing? How do you know? What clues tell you so?

Could it have been any other instrument, too?

Story 2

Dad was on a ladder building shelves and he'd been at it for ages. Luka came up the stairs, carefully carrying a tray. 'My word that's a welcome sight!', Dad said. 'This is thirsty work.'

What did Luka bring up to his Dad? How do you know? What clues tell you so?

What else might it have been?

Reading Between the Lines Set Two

Story 3

The school was planting a tree. All the children had taken turns to dig out a trowel full of earth. Now Mr Williams was making quicker progress as he dug out huge clods of earth and tossed them up on the side. He was soon standing in quite a deep hole.

What was Mr Williams using to make the hole? How do you know? What clues tell you so?

Story 4

By half way down the hill Tessa's tyre was absolutely flat. 'Only a slow puncture', said Pat. 'Here, blow it up as hard as you can and it should get us home.'

What did Pat pass to Tessa? How do you know? What clues tell you so?

Story 5

'Nothing wrong with his legs or his paws', said the vet reassuringly. 'Just his nails have got too long.' He reached for his instrument case and in no time the job was done. Monty's walking was back to normal as Ben led him home.

What did the vet use on Monty's nails? How do you know? What clues tell you so?

What had Ben thought was the matter with Monty? Why might he have thought so?

Story 6

Gran wasn't taking much part in the conversation. Mum looked at her and passed her something in a little box. Gran fiddled with her ear for a minute and then gave a broad smile. 'That's better', she said 'Now you'll have to watch what you say about me.'

What did Mum bring Gran? How do you know? What clues tell you so?

Part 1 - Instrument

Story 7

The mechanic was fixing Grandpa's electric wheelchair. When he had finished he gave them a grin. 'I know your Grandpa drives like Jenson Button', he said. 'So I've put something on the handle to warn pedestrians to get out of his way. They'll jump out of their skins!'

What do you think the mechanic has put on Grandpa's wheelchair? How do you know? What clues tell you so?

Do you think anyone would really do this?

Story 8

A group from Year 7 were in the Science Room. This week they were looking at insects' wings. When it was Becky's turn, she looked into the eyepiece, adjusted the focus and gasped with amazement at the colours and the patterns.

What was Becky using? How do you know? What clues tell you so?

Story 9

When Annie's finger nails had been filed and lotion rubbed into her hands, it was time to choose the colour. Annie chose deep red and decided as well to have a flower on one finger of each hand. The manicurist picked up the bottle, and set to work.

What was the manicurist using? How do you know? What clues tell you so?

Story 10

'Now', said Mum, as she finished putting the picnic things in the basket. 'This one has hot soup in and this one has iced coca cola. Don't mix them up!'

What were the last things Mum put into the picnic basket? How do you know? What clues tell you so?

Reading Between the Lines Set Two

Story 11

'While we're waiting for the new cooker to arrive, we'll just have to make do with this', said Jamie. 'Thank goodness we brought it to the flat with us.' He popped the two mugs in, pressed the button for '40 seconds' and handed his steaming soup to Andy.

What was Jamie using? How do you know? What clues tell you so?

Story 12

The college lawns looked as if they had been trimmed with nail scissors and painted green, they were so perfect and they were patterned with broad stripes. One of the gardeners was still finishing off in the distance.

What was the gardener using? How do you know? What clues tell you so?

Place

Level 1	**50**
Level 2	**53**
Level 3	**55**
Level 4	**57**

Reading Between the Lines Set Two

Level 1

Spot the clues that tell you WHERE IT IS OR WHERE IT HAPPENS.

Clues might be about:

- Places
- What you can see
- What you can hear or feel

Here is an example. The clues are in bold type.

The doorbell rang. 'At last', thought Mum. The **driver** brought the crates in and unloaded the bags onto the floor. When he'd gone, she made a coffee before unpacking **this week's load**. She grouped the contents of the bags accordingly – things for the **fridge**, things for the **freezer**, stuff to go in the **cupboard**, **pet food**, **cleaning products** and fresh **fruit** and **veg**. The next job was to put it all away before she had to do the school run. In half an hour the fridge was full, there was hardly any space in the store cupboard and she'd had to re-arrange the **cupboard under the sink**.

Where was Mum? How do we know? What clues tell you so?

- *A supermarket delivery has arrived*
- *In this room, there is a fridge, a freezer, cupboards*
- *Mum needs to put away all the things that have been delivered*

   = Mum must be in the kitchen

Part 1 - Place

Story 1

Rick and his Dad and his Uncle Dave caught the 10 o'clock train. From Waterloo, they took the Jubilee Line. It took about 20 minutes to walk from their stop and Rick noticed lots of other people were going in the same direction. They showed their **tickets** at the **gate** and made their way to the **East Stand**. 'Five minutes till **kick-off**', said his Dad as they found their seats. Rick felt very proud to be standing by his Dad and Uncle Dave, wearing the brand new **strip** he had got for his birthday.

Where are Rick and his Dad and Uncle? How do you know? What clues tell you so?

Story 2

Meena bundled her clothes into the **wire basket** and pushed it into the **locker**. The **tiles were wet** and a bit slippery as she made her way to join the others at the far end. 'Help!', she thought as she looked at the distance to the other end. Somehow, from here, it looked even further. She could see her Mum and little sister waving from the spectators' balcony. As she waved back, she suddenly felt determined. A little voice in her head said 'Come on Meena, you can do it, it's only **25 metres**, that's the same as **two widths**.'

Where is Meena? How do you know? What clues tell you so?

Story 3

'Why does this place always have such an effect on the twins', thought Laura as she grabbed Olly by the back of his shirt, narrowly avoiding him crashing into an elderly man who was busy choosing a **tin of soup**. Meanwhile, Joe was running and sliding on the smooth tiles in the **vegetable aisle**. In desperation, Laura bundled both boys into the **trolley** and headed for the **checkout**.

Where is Laura? How do you know? What clues tell you so?

Reading Between the Lines Set Two

Story 4

Jamilla loved being in here helping Grandad. One of her favourite things was sorting the **packets of seeds**. Different piles for **vegetables** and **flowers**. Grandad kept the place very tidy. All the tools had their place on a hook on the wall. The **pots** were stacked according to size and kept on a shelf. The **mower, wheelbarrow and watering can** stood in a neat row at one end. At the other end was a cupboard where Grandad kept books and **gardening magazines**.

Where are Jamilla and Grandad? How do you know? What clues tell you so?

Story 5

'At last!', thought Mel as she unscrewed her radio aerial and tapped in the code. She started the engine and slowly drove forwards until the STOP sign appeared. Soon the **car was covered in foam** and the **huge brushes beat against the windows**. Mel tried not to think about the time when the brushes had failed to move off the **windscreen** and she'd had to keep her hand on the horn until the **forecourt attendant** came and turned the whole thing off.

Where is Mel? How do you know? What clues tell you so?

Story 6

Harry and Josh could hear the music getting louder as they trudged up the hill. As they approached the entrance, they could smell **burgers and hot dogs**. Just inside the barrier there were lots of different **stalls** trying to persuade you to spend your money in the hope of **winning a large fluffy toy**. However, the boys had more exciting things in mind and headed straight for the most impressive one of all, right over at the far end of the field. Imagine their disappointment when the young man taking the money said you had to be **over 1.5 metres tall** to go on this one.

Where were Harry and Josh? How do you know? What clues tell you so?

Part 1 - Place

Level 2

Story 1

'Starts at 2, c u outside', texted Luca to his friend Pavel. He got there early, of course. Luca was always early. While he waited he wondered if it would be **as good as the book**. At last, Pavel appeared, only minutes before it began. No time even to buy **popcorn**. By the time they got in there were only a few **seats** left but at least they could sit together. 'Wish we had some sweets', muttered Pavel as the **lights dimmed**.

Where are Luca and Pavel? How do you know? What clues tell you so?

Story 2

Laura Curtis put on her **trainers** and led the class down the corridor. Once inside, she divided them into four groups. 'Quiet now, 4A', she called. 'This term we are going to concentrate on developing **flexibility**, **strength**, **control and balance**. Today you will need **mats**, **benches** and **beanbags**.' As the class began assembling the equipment, Laura glanced at the end wall. 'We are NOT using the **bars** today Jasper! Get down at once!'

Where are Laura and her class? How do you know? What clues tell you so?

Story 3

Mel loved this part. It was so exciting, getting up really, really early. Then parking the car and pulling the **suitcases** across the cold carpark, lit by blueish white lights. Once inside there was so much to take in. First, the lining up at the desk and getting rid of the bags. Then, the **departure lounge** with all its shops. Mum disappeared immediately and came back a bit later looking slightly guilty with a small, expensive looking bag on her arm. Dad kept peering up at the board and finally said, 'Nearly there, **we're boarding in 10 minutes**.'

Where is Mel and her family? How do you know? What clues tell you so?

Reading Between the Lines Set Two

Story 4

Mum was reading the map. 'OK', she said. 'Take the next right.' They turned into a narrow rutted track and bumped along for a while. 'Are you sure this is right?', muttered Dad. Finally, they came to a gateway that had a weathered sign saying **'Welcome to Spindleberry Farm.'** The track was even bumpier here but eventually they arrived at a little shed. Dad told the lady: 'We've come **for the week**, family of four.' She looked in her diary and said, 'Got it, you're in **number 14, sleeps 4,** just over there on the left.' 'Well', said Mum, 'at least we **don't have to put it up!'**

Where are the family? How do you know? What clues tell you so?

Story 5

Luca looked out of the window. Everything looked grey and raindrops streaked the glass. Through the droplets, he made out fields, bushes, sometimes roads and sheep and cows huddled together. Luca glanced at Mum who was busy on her phone as usual. Down the aisle he spotted their big purple **suitcase**, perched in the **baggage space**. The door at the end opened and a man came through pushing **a trolley with drinks and crisps** and things. Luca poked his Mum, looking hopeful. No luck, she just smiled down at him. 'Hey, Luca, **only two stops to go!'**

Where are Luca and his mum? How do you know? What clues tell you so?

Story 6

Ricky felt a bit nervous even though the man in **the white coat** had sounded quite jolly and encouraging. 'OK, old man, let's get you up a bit higher, then I can have a proper look!' Rick didn't really like lying on his back like a stuck beetle while the man poked spiky **metal things** in his **mouth**. The man muttered things to the girl who stood holding a tray of sharp looking objects. Finally, he looked at Rick's mother and said: 'Well done, Mum, you've taught this boy to look after them. **Beautiful set of gnashers!'**

Where is Rick? How do you know? What clues tell you so?

Part 1 - Place

Level 3

In the next stories, you have to *find the clues yourself*.

Story 1

Six-year-old Zack stamped his foot and stood with his head down, arms folded. 'Not fair', he muttered while 10-ten-year-old sister rolled her eyes and pointed to the sign that said 'Over 8s Only'. She had a slight smile on her face as she queued for the 'MegaZap Experience'. Mum tried to smooth things over by suggesting to Zack that they try for the 'Zoomerooma'. This didn't go down well with Zack who retorted 'No way, Mum, it's just for toddlers!'

Where are Zack and his sister? How do you know? What clues tell you so?

Story 2

Carrying the basket carefully, she crossed the field behind the house. It was a hot day and she was glad to go through the gap in the hedge. Here, it was cool and shaded. Underfoot, there were crunchy leaves on the winding path. A few flowers grew in the spaces that let the sunlight through. She stopped to pick some, listening to the birds high in the branches. She looked around at the tall trunks, the first branches high up, way out of reach.

Where is the girl? How do you know? What clues tell you so?

Story 3

Even though it was a chilly, windy day, there were several families shielded by rocks or windbreaks. Some young boys were flying kites and down near the breaking foam a few brave children were paddling. Above the constant hiss of water pulling on shingle, you could hear birds, shrieking into the wind. If you walked along to the rocks at the far end, there were endless pools teeming with creatures.

Where is this? How do you know? What clues tell you so?

Reading Between the Lines Set Two

Story 4

Harvey pulled his hoodie up to keep the rain off. Cars, lorries and taxis swished by throwing up spray on the glass panel. The man at the front was studying the timetable and looking a bit worried. After a bit he turned and asked Harvey's Nan 'Does this one stop at Kensal Rise?' 'No love, that's the 52 you'll be wanting. Next stop down the road.' At that moment, the next one pulled up. 'At last', sighed Nan as she and Harvey got on and showed their passes.

Where are Harvey and his Nan? How do you know? What clues tell you so?

Story 5

On Saturdays, Magda and Pavel earned a bit of pocket money helping out. Today Magda was chopping courgettes and Pavel was washing some lettuce for a salad. The big wide pan was sizzling away and Mum was wiping her hands on her apron before tackling the pastry dough. She passed a large bowl to Magda to put in the sink and picked up the wooden rolling pin. Soon a delicious smell of frying garlic rose from the pan. 'Not long till lunch', thought Pavel!

Where are Pavel and Magda? How do you know? What clues tell you so?

Story 6

Lara and her friend Ellie were so excited. At last the day had arrived! Lara's sister had helped them buy the tickets online ages ago and now they were actually HERE! They queued patiently and waited while their bags were checked by security. After what seemed ages, they followed the crowd down the narrow corridor that led to the arena. It was huge, much bigger than the girls were expecting. 'Wow, El, I can't believe we're actually here! Do you realize that in exactly 15 minutes she'll be out there, on stage, in front of us!'

Where are Lara and Ellie? How do you know? What clues tell you so?

Part 1 - Place

Level 4

Story 1

There was a queue at the Reception counter, so she was told to 'Login on the screen'. Martha Picket looked around the waiting room, bewildered. A very young looking nurse touched her arm and said: 'Over there, you tap the screen, put in your name and date of birth so they know you are here.'

Where is Martha? How do you know? What clues tell you so?

Story 2

It was much bigger than Jay was expecting. There were several aisles selling bedding, foods, toys and other equipment. It wasn't till you got past these you could find the actual animals, carefully penned in clean wire cages of varying sizes.

Where was Jay? How do you know? What clues tell you so?

Story 3

It was the moment Aziz had always dreaded. After his shy knock, the door opened and the tall, menacing figure of Mr Fanshawe towered above him. 'Aziz, isn't it?', he said. 'Fighting in the playground wasn't it? Again.'

Where do you think Aziz is? What makes you think that? What clues tell you so?

Reading Between the Lines Set Two

Story 4

Granny always brought her here on Saturday mornings. 'Right, Leah', she said. 'You go and choose yours from the Children's Corner while I have a look through the Crime section.' Leah loved reading and found it quite hard to only choose four titles.

Where are Leah and her Granny? How do you know? What clues tell you so?

Story 5

This was the best school trip ever! Ellie looked in amazement at the completely different world on the other side of the glass. Of course, she'd seen them all before in pictures but watching them glide gracefully in and out of the swaying weed was magical.

Where do you think Ellie is? What do you think the creatures might be? What clues tell you so?

Story 6

Janet and her sister walked slowly, in silence, heads bent down, scanning the tide lines. They'd been doing this right here since they were children and the thrill of finding them never diminished. Straightening up for a moment Janet said 'Look, do you think that's a seal?'

Where are the two sisters? What clues tell you so?

Part 1 - Place

Story 7

'Right', said Ben. 'It says three hours is £1.20. How long do you think we are going to need?' Julie, his wife, said 'Well, by the time we've bought the present and had lunch, I reckon we'd better get three hours' worth. There's some change in that box thing in the front of the car, I'll nip back and get it.'

Where are Ben and Julie? What clues tell you so?

Story 8

Josh was watching TV when suddenly he heard a funny noise, a sort of trickling sound. It seemed to be coming from upstairs. Then he remembered and leapt out of the chair and galloped up the stairs. Oh no, it was all over the floor and seeping under the door. He ran to the tap to turn it off.

Where did Josh run to? What clues tell you so?

Story 9

'Are we nearly there?', whined Billy from the back seat. 'We've only just left home', replied Dad, glancing in the mirror before overtaking a huge lorry. 'If the traffic's not too bad, we should be there by teatime. Why don't you look out of the window and see how many yellow cars you can spot.'

Where are Billy and his Dad? What clues tell you so?

Reading Between the Lines Set Two

Story 10

Dad was right. It was 5 o'clock when they drove through the gates and up the drive. Billy was excited. 'Wow, there's a playground AND a swimming pool! Can we go for a swim right now?' Dad said they had to go to Reception first to find where their tent was.

Where are Billy and his Dad? How do you know? What clues tell you so?

Story 11

Mina Patel finally got to the counter. It was always busy on Tuesdays, with people collecting their pensions. She put her parcel on the scales. 'First or second class?', asked the assistant. 'First please,' replied Mina. 'And a book of second class stamps please.'

Where is Mina? How do you know? What clues tell you so?

Story 12

'Time to check your highlights, Fern', called Abbi, the manageress. 'Back in a minute', said Fern to the lady she was blow-drying. She crossed the salon and undid a couple of Mrs Fletcher's foils. 'About five more minutes Mrs F', she said.

Where do you think Fern works? How do you know? What clues tell you so?

Occupation

Level 1	**62**
Level 2	**65**
Level 3	**67**
Level 4	**70**

Reading Between the Lines Set Two

Level 1

Spot the clues that tell you WHAT SOMEONE'S JOB OR HOBBY IS.

Clues might be about:

- Where they work
- What they like doing
- What sort of work they are doing
- What they are making

Here is an example. The clues are in bold type.

Bill had arrived at the **depot** just in time for a cup of tea before he set off. He picked up the keys, put on his **cap** and climbed into the **driver's seat**. The first stop was at the end of River Street. They climbed in, pushing and shoving as usual. Bill **glanced in his mirror**, making sure they were all sitting down with their belts done up. Then he pulled out into the rush hour traffic and made his way along to Park Vale where there was a long queue of impatient **youngsters**. He was just about to pull away when he saw a boy of about 11, running as fast as he could towards him. With a sigh, Bill **opened the door** again. 'You need to get up a bit earlier, sonny', he said. 'That's the second time you've been late this week!' They finally arrived at **Parkway Academy** and Bill watched with a smile as they trouped through the gates, just before the **bell went**.

What is Bill's job? How do you know? What clues tell you so?

- *He goes to the depot*
- *He wears a cap*
- *He gets into the driver's seat*
- *He looks in his mirror*
- *He stops at Parkway Academy*
    = *He must be a school bus driver*

Part 1 - Occupation

Story 1

Alina looked at her watch and sighed. Another five and a half hours till the **end of her shift**. It was filling up now, as people stopped to **shop on their way home** from work. Alina recognized the next customer – she often came in her on a Monday evening. Smart suit, good haircut, obviously had a well-paid job. The woman deposited the contents of her **basket** on the **belt** and Alina started **processing the items through the till**. 'Do you **need any bags** today?', she asked the woman when everything had gone through.

What is Alina's job? How do you know? What clues tell you so?

Story 2

Dave put on his **greasy blue overalls**, ready to start a day's work. First, he had to check the **brakes** on Mrs Drake's **Nissan Micra**. Then there were a couple of **MOTs** and a full service on an **Audi**. Today was a bit more taxing because he also had a work experience boy from the local secondary school. He was a shy-looking boy called Josh. 'Right, Josh', said Dave. 'What do you know about **car engines**?'

What do you think Dave's job is? How do you know? What clues tell you so?

Story 3

Saturday nights were always really busy and tonight was no exception. Carlo was boiling hot as he stood **chopping onions and ginger** as fast as he could. His chocolate and lime surprise was chilling in the fridge and he had to serve **10 plates of 'Sea Bass Orientale'** in the next five minutes. The **pans sizzled**, timers bleeped and Ramon, the boss was yelling at everyone to hurry up. Carlo scraped the onions and ginger into the pan and shouted: '**Two minutes, Chef**'

What is Carlo's job? How do you know? What clues tell you so?

Copyright material from Catherine Delamain & Jill Spring (2018), *Reading Between the Lines Set Two*, Routledge

63

Reading Between the Lines Set Two

Story 4

On the way to the job, Pete had to get a **concrete mixer** from the hire centre. He loaded it into the back of his **van** and set off. The blocks should already have been delivered and the **scaffolding** was up, so he could get straight on with **building the outside walls**. He just hoped Taz would be there to do the **labouring**, otherwise it was going to take twice as long. If he could just get the outside walls up today before the weather changed, he could put a big tarpaulin over the top.

What is Pete's job? How do you know? What clues tell you so?

Story 5

'Right, that's the **laminating done**', said Ellie, picking up the sheets. She cut them up into individual cards and took them across to the **classroom**. Matt Talbot looked up as she walked in. 'Goodness knows how he's going to cope today, what with it being **Sports Day** and the Awards Ceremony.' 'Don't worry, Matt, I've made **some picture cards** to show him what's happening', replied Ellie as the children came into **class**. 'Finn, hi, come over here and let's see what we're doing today', said Ellie, putting the little pictures in order across the table.

What is Ellie's job? How do you know? What clues tell you so?

Story 6

'Excuse me', said the woman at **table seven**. 'We've been waiting 20 minutes for the **meals we ordered** and nothing seems to be happening.' Andreas smiled politely at the couple and checked his **order pad**. 'I'm so sorry, Madam That was **two steak and chips** with side salad, correct?' The woman nodded, without smiling. 'I'll go and check with the kitchen right away', continued Andreas. He made his way across the dining room, **collecting empty plates and glasses** as he went.

What is Andreas' job? How do you know? What clues tell you so?

Part 1 - Occupation

Level 2

Story 1

Mark trudged out to the garage to load up the van. It looked like a busy day, starting with Mrs Cuthbertson's **lawn**. After that he had to cut Dr Patel's **front hedge** and plant out old Miss Elliot's **bedding plants**. Then if he had time he'd pop round to Mary Fish and help her put in some new roses and probably take her garden rubbish to the tip. Busy, but Mark loved it, being out in the open all day, **planting seeds**, watching things grow and taking care of so many gardens.

What do you think Mark's job is? How do you know? What clues tell you so?

Story 2

The make-up artist put the final touches to Galla's face. Galla looked in the mirror. She looked fine: smooth, sleek hair and a flawless complexion. The simple but beautifully cut navy blue dress really suited her. But inside she felt nervous. She'd been the 'side-kick' on this **show** several times but never had to **present it** herself. What if the guests were really difficult to speak to? What if she dried up completely and couldn't think of anything to say? She took a deep breath, walked into the **studio** and prepared to **face the cameras**.

What is Galla's job? How do you know? What clues tell you so?

Reading Between the Lines Set Two

Story 3

From the age of about eight, when he was given his first **violin**, Jonas had always practised for at least two hours a day. At the age of 14, he won a scholarship to the **Royal College of Music** and, by 18, was winning competitions all over the country. Jonas lived for music and never tired of the amazing applause from the **audience** at the end of a **concert**. Now he was accepted as a professional and travelled all over the world giving concerts. There was something magic about sitting in the **orchestra pit** and waiting for the moment when the **conductor appeared** and silence fell.

What is Jonas' job? How do you know? What clues tell you so?

Story 4

'I've dropped my bunny', wailed a little boy as Anton started on the drugs round. He paused his trolley and found the little velvet rabbit down the side of the **child's bed**. 'Don't worry, Ben. Look here he is and your mum and dad will be back very soon.' Anton loved his job but he hated seeing **sick children** with no one to be with them. At that moment, the **Ward Sister** appeared, checking that everything was going to plan. 'No worries, Sister', said Anton, knowing that although she seemed a bit fierce she was committed to making those children's stay as good as possible.

What is Anton's job? How do you know? What clues tell you so?

Story 5

It was nearly midnight when Bianca finally finished the marking and she hadn't even planned tomorrow's **science lesson**. She fell into bed and dreamt that Freddie Pontin had opened the tank with the stick insects inside and lots of them had escaped. It was almost a relief to wake at 6.15 and realize that all she had to do was drive the 20 miles **to Millbrook First**. Then she remembered it was Wednesday and it was her turn to do **assembly**.

What is Bianca's job? How do you know? What clues tell you so?

Part 1 - Occupation

Story 6

Jacko put on his colours, weighed in and walked to the **stable** area. Over The Moon **whinnied** when he spotted Jacko. They had a little while to warm up before the **race** so Jacko mounted and made his way to the warm-up **paddock**. Several of the others were already there, some quiet, some a bit jumpy. Over The Moon seemed keen and eager today, unlike last week's meeting when he'd refused the first fence. A whistle sounded and the **riders made their way to the starting gate**. 'Come on, Over, this time we're going to be first', whispered Jacko.

What is Jacko's job? How do you know? What clues tell you so?

Level 3

In the next stories, you have to *find the clues yourself*.

Story 1

Eddie climbed into the cab and set off up the hill. It was a fine day and he was hoping to get the top field ploughed ready for the spring crops. If he could finish the ploughing by midday he should be able to go into town and pick up some cattle feed before his monthly visit from the accountant to check the books. Luckily, his son, Ben, was home from college and had offered to do the milking tonight.

What is Eddie's job? How do you know? What clues tell you so?

Reading Between the Lines Set Two

Story 2

Simba's shift started at 2 pm. First, he checked the incident book to see what had been happening so far. Then he and his colleague, Jim, set off in the patrol car. There had been another break-in at Beaumont Terrace and Simba had an idea who might be able to help him with some enquiries. As they turned the corner into the Terrace he noticed a scruffy-looking white van that looked as if it had been abandoned. He made a note to check it out later, after he'd had a word with the lad who lived at Number 24.

What is Simba's job? How do you know? What clues tell you so?

Story 3

'Right, stand back everyone and let me have a proper look', said Rob. A motorbike had collided with a car and there was broken glass in the road. On the grass verge, a man with a helmet lay curled up. Rob knelt down and spoke calmly and gently to him. 'Don't worry, mate', he said. 'We'll soon get you sorted out.' He carefully examined the man while his colleague fetched the stretcher.

What is Rob's job? How do you know? What clues tell you so?

Story 4

Alf watched the passengers climbing on board. Most of them were quite elderly so it took quite a long time. Once they were all seated Alf put on his cap and climbed the steps. 'Good morning, ladies and gentlemen! Welcome to Greenbank Tours! Our first stop will be in about an hour, at Little Fording, where you will have a chance to stretch your legs. Then it's on to the Black Dog, where we will be stopping for lunch. Our tour of the castle starts at 2.30 and takes about an hour. Does anyone have any questions?'

What is Alf's job? How do you know? What clues tell you so?

Part 1 - Occupation

Story 5

It was 6.45 am and Mike was loading up the van. His first call was to fit a new dishwasher at a house on the other side of town. He made sure he had all the right tools and equipment and checked his mobile for any new messages. As usual, there were several, all expecting him to come immediately. He looked to see if any were really urgent. A distraught sounding woman had left a muddled sort of message: 'It's pouring down the stairs now', she moaned. Mike sighed. He'd have to contact the dishwasher owner and explain that he'd got to deal with an emergency first.

What is Mike's job? How do you know? What clues tell you so?

Story 6

'Georgie Phipps stop pushing! You need to wait your turn just like everyone else', grumbled Janice Simms as she handed the next portion to a little girl in Year 2. The little girl didn't looked pleased. 'Miss, it's got green bits in it', she complained. 'Come on, now, that's good and healthy', replied Janice. 'Go on, give it a try – you might find you like it after all!' It took at least 15 minutes to serve them all and by that time the first lot were coming back for second helpings.

What is Janice's job? How do you know? What clues tell you so?

Reading Between the Lines Set Two

Level 4

Story 1

Dave Briggs looked around the space that would be the new kitchen. Mrs Banford stood anxiously waiting for him to say something. 'So, Mrs B, where do you want the plug sockets? And how many exactly? Also, do you need a socket for a TV in here as well?

What is Dave's job? How do you know? What clues tell you so?

Story 2

Bob had already measured the space for the oak worktops. He'd collected the wood so now he needed to cut the pieces to fit. The electrician and plumber had finished their work so it was down to Bob to finally put the brand new oak kitchen together.

What is Bob's job? How do you know? What clues tell you so?

Story 3

It was 8.50 and the waiting room was already full. Matt looked at his computer. First was someone called Eddie Sandhurst. He glanced through the previous records, noting *hip pain, rash on upper arm, dry cough*.

What is Matt's job? How do you know? What clues tell you so?

Story 4

Leon stood at one end. 'Hi, Magpies, lovely to see you all. Line up along the side and listen carefully. Today we are going to try some real front crawl, so remember what I told you about coordinating breathing, arm and leg movements!'

What is Leon's job? How do you know? What clues tell you so?

Part 1 - Occupation

Story 5

Anya shivered in a sleeveless shift dress. Today they were shooting the ballroom scene. 'Glamorous!', she muttered to herself. 'Getting up at 5.30 and hanging around for the crew to arrive to shoot the scene is anything but!'

What is Anya's job? How do you know? What clues tell you so?

Story 6

JoJo felt nervous. There was a big crowd out there and they were on in five minutes. Ed, the lead guitar, had only just turned up and there was something wrong with the sound system. 'Come on JJ', he said to himself. 'You know the lyrics, you love the song, just let them have it!

What is JoJo's job? How do you know? What clues tell you so?

Story 7

Farouk walked across the tarmac, climbing the stairs and took his place in the cockpit. Visibility was good today and they were due to take off on time. He did the usual checks and waited for the signal to taxi to the runway.

What is Farouk's job? How do you know? What clues tell you so?

Story 8

'Right, boss, got it', said Robyn. 'I'm meeting him in the bar at the Clarence and finding out all I can about the Bentham House fire story.' The story was going to be printed in tomorrow's edition so Robyn knew she had to get going quickly.

What is Robyn's job? How do you know? What clues tell you so?

Reading Between the Lines Set Two

Story 9

When Jenna arrived at work, the first thing she heard was a constant whimpering sound. She quickly went out to the kennel area and saw the little terrier who'd had the operation yesterday. He barked hopefully when he saw Jenna. 'Don't worry, Buster, as soon as Mr Taylor has checked the stitches we'll let you out.'

What is Jenna's job? How do you know? What clues tell you so?

Story 10

'I want a completely new style', said the woman, looking in the mirror and flicking her hair this way and that. Layla leafed through a styles magazine and made a few suggestions. 'Can you do this one?', said the woman, pointing to an asymmetrical bob with a straight fringe.

What is Layla's job? How do you know? What clues tell you so?

Story 11

'Can you help me, young man?', said an elderly lady. Finn asked how he could help. 'Well my son bought it but it's all too complicated. All I want to do is make phone calls on it.' Finn looked at the device. 'Don't worry', he said, 'I can sort it out so you don't get confused by all the extras. That's what we are here for!'

What is Finn's job? How do you know? What clues tell you so?

Story 12

Matt had a rule. 'Write for two hours a day, minimum. Doesn't matter what, you can always edit it.' Maybe this was how he'd won 'Crime Bestseller of the Year'. He sat down and looked at the blank new page on his laptop.

What is Matt's job? How do you know? What clues tell you so?

Categories

Level 1   74

Level 2   77

Level 3   80

Level 4   83

Level 1

Spot the clues that tell you what GROUP OR CATEGORY OF THINGS THIS IS ABOUT.

Clues might be about:

- What it looks like
- What you do with it
- Where you find it
- What it's for

Here's an example. The clues are in bold type.

Harry had always loved them. Even when he was only about two he could tell you all their long, **complicated names**. His Granny had given him a set of the most well-known ones for his birthday. He used to spend ages, separating the '**meat eaters**' from the '**plant eaters**'. When he was about six, Granny took him to a special **museum**, by the seaside in **Dorset**. Harry was amazed because here they had actual **skeletons** of the creatures that had **inhabited the earth** all those years ago.

What kind of creature is this about? How do you know?

- *Small children like these little plastic toys*
- *They often have long difficult names*
- *There are skeletons of them in a museum by the sea in Dorset*
- *They lived on Earth many years ago*
  - *= The creatures must be dinosaurs*

Part 1 - Categories

Story 1

Jez pulled on his boots and picked up the **lead**. 'Come on, Dizzy', he called. 'Let's go to the park.' They set off up the hill and soon reached the tall iron gates. 'I'll **let you off** once we are past the children's playground', said Jez. It was a chilly autumn morning and already the leaves beginning to blow across the path. Jez was just about to **unclip** the **lead** when he noticed a young woman **being tugged along**. 'Wow, **what a monster!**', he commented, hoping Dizzy would behave.

What is Dizzy? How do you know? What clues tell you so?

Story 2

Amir was with his Mum and Dad in a furniture shop. It was a huge great place and it felt like they had been there for ages. Why couldn't his parents just make their minds up, he thought, feeling very, very bored. They couldn't seem to agree about anything. Mum wanted the **squashy, comfy kind**. Dad wanted something with a special **button to alter the position of the back**. 'I don't like that one', said Mum 'It hasn't got enough **cushions** and the colour won't match the **sofa** at home.' 'Hey, look over here', replied Dad. 'These three are on offer, just the right colour and you can choose your own cushions.'

What are Amir's parents buying? How do you know? What clues tell you so?

Story 3

Lennie and his cousin, Reg, walked into the showroom. Almost immediately, a smartly dressed young man came over. 'What can I interest you in sir?', he said to Lennie. 'Well, at this stage, we're just having a look, if that's OK', replied Lennie. 'Just let me know if I can help with anything', said the salesman, returning to his desk. 'Wow, Len, look at the **alloys** on that one!' Reg was bending over to inspect the **gleaming metal**. '**Not enough room in the boot**, though', answered Lennie. 'Not now that we've got to fit the buggy and the seat in.' 'But this is more like it', he continued, peering into the **driving seat** before opening the back doors.

What are Lennie and Reg looking at? How do you know? What clues tell you so?

Reading Between the Lines Set Two

Story 4

It was a bright morning in early May. 'My very favourite time of year', thought Ally as she walked through her garden. She collected what she needed from the **shed** and stepped into the **greenhouse**. Four of the trays were ready so she lined up the **pots** on the bench and filled them up. Using a pencil she made three holes in each pot. She took down the first tray and began **carefully lifting them** one by one with an old spoon. Each one was placed in one of the holes and the **soil** firmed up around them. By the time she'd finished all four trays, it was late morning and Ally was hungry. She closed the **greenhouse** and went back into the house.

What kind of thing was Ally putting in the pots? How do you know? What clues tell you so?

Story 5

Every morning during the cold winter months, Ned Willis fed them. He collected old **crusts of bread** that he **crumbled onto the grass**. He filled the **feeders with seeds and peanuts** and made sure the ice was broken in the stone dish. Today there was frost on the grass and a cold wind blowing. Ned went back into his kitchen and made a cup of tea. There was a chair by the big window that looked straight onto the garden. Ned kept a pair of **binoculars** on the chair. He settled down with his cup of tea and waited. After a few minutes, they started to appear, **pecking** hungrily at the **seeds**. Ned picked up the binoculars to get a closer look. He identified four different **species** today.

What was Ned feeding in his garden? How do you know? What clues tell you so?

Part 1 - Categories

Story 6

Max loved going into Grandad's workshop. Grandad kept everything very neat and tidy. There were little boxes stacked on the shelves, labelled in Grandad's sloping handwriting. **Nails. Screws (short). Screws (long). Tap washers.** Today, Grandad was opening a large wooden box. 'Come on Max', he said. 'Help me sort this lot out. It's all got in a bit of a muddle.' They set to work, taking each item out of the box and placing them on **the work bench**. 'What are they all for, Grandad?', asked Max. 'Well, this one is for **banging in nails**. And this electric one **makes holes in walls**. These are for putting **screws** in – there are five different sizes. And if you need to **undo a nut** you'll need one of these. Careful with that, Max, it's very sharp. We might need it later when **we cut the wood** for your farm.'

What are Max and Grandad sorting out in the workshop? How do you know? What clues tell you so?

Level 2

Story 1

'So, that's our theme for this year's stall at the Community Festival', concluded Evelina Harris. The Community Festival was held every year in the Town Hall and included all kinds of crafts, musicians, local produce and contributions from local schools. Evelina was the chairman of the Homestrust project, which encouraged people in the community to share ideas and skills. 'You can pick **fresh ones from your gardens**, make them out of **felt, knit or crochet them** or even submit drawings and paintings. The idea is to have as many different kind of **blooms** as possible.'

What is the Homestrust theme this year? How do you know? What clues tell you so?

Reading Between the Lines Set Two

Story 2

Ellie and her family were on holiday in Devon. Today was special because Ellie and her Nan were going off for the day by themselves. No Mum and Dad or annoying little brothers. 'Right, Ellie', said Nan. 'We've got three different ones to visit and the first one is right here in the village.' Ellie looked across the village green and saw the **tall spire** sticking up into the air. Inside, it was **cool and peaceful**. Ellie gazed up at the **great stone arches** and the **huge windows filled with coloured glass**. Nan beckoned to her and showed her the **carved angels** on the ends of the wooden **pews**.

What kind of places is Ellie visiting with her Nan? How do you know? What clues tell you so?

Story 3

Jill and Jennie walked up the drive to the magnificent country house. They waited with the other visitors in the Great Hall. Soon, the guide arrived and gave them a short history of the house and its owners before taking them round the rooms. 'Most of the ones in this room are **members of the family**', she explained. 'The **one of Elizabeth the First** is, of course, a very **well-known image**', she went on. Jill nudged Jennie and pointed to the end wall. 'Wherever you stand, **he's looking at you**', she whispered. When the tour was finished, they both decided they liked the watercolours of the lake and woods the best.

What kind of things are they looking at? How do you know? What clues tell you so?

Part 1 - Categories

Story 4

Irina felt nervous as she waited for the bus. Finally, it arrived and she clambered on, trying hard not to bash anyone with the big **case**. She had to take up two seats, one for her and one for the case, because it was too big for the overhead lockers or the luggage storage. Her friend Izzie got on at the next stop, sitting in front of Irina with her **canvas bag on** her lap. By the time they reached the Town Hall, there were several other students with various **bags and cases**. They filed off the bus and crossed the road to the Town Hall. Inside the entrance was a sign that said '**Grade 5 exams** First Floor, Room 6.'

What are the students carrying to the Town Hall? How do you know? What clues tell you so?

Story 5

Anne-Marie loved helping in her Auntie Kay's shop on Saturdays. Auntie Kay said when she was old enough she could have a proper Saturday job and get paid. 'We've got a busy day today, Anne-Marie', said Kay as she took a **fresh batch** out of the **oven**. 'Could you put all the **sliced ones** on the top shelf, brown at one end, white at the other? Then the **baguettes** need to be put in that deep basket, upright. When you've done that this batch of bloomers should be cool enough to go in the window.' She then disappeared back to the kitchen where a huge **bowl of dough** sat proving by the oven. Anne-Marie got to work, loving the warm smell of the **yeast** and the floury **crusts** of the bloomers.

What does Auntie Kay sell in her shop? How do you know? What clues tell you so?

Reading Between the Lines Set Two

Story 6

Marco lifted the rack of cups, mugs and glasses out of the dishwasher. He made sure they were all dry and arranged them along the shelf behind the counter. Franco turned the sign to 'Open' and unlocked the door. In no time, a long queue had formed at the counter. Franco scribbled down the **orders** and passed them to Marco. The first one was all hot – **two blacks**, **one small white** and one large. Next was a mother with three small boys. Two of them wanted **fizzy**, the other **flat**. After that there were a couple of young women on a shopping spree. 'Let's have one of those, just for a treat, with a scoop of ice cream and a little umbrella', said the taller woman. Marco stirred them carefully, **dropped in a scoop of vanilla** ice cream and floated a pink umbrella in one and a blue in the other.

What is Marco making? How do you know? What clues tell you so?

Level 3

In the next stories, you have to *find the clues yourself.*

Story 1

As soon as he got home from school Jez changed into his kit. The new trainers felt great and he was looking forward to a game with his friend, Finn. Picking up his bag, he set off across town to the new ground. Finn was already there warming up when Jez arrived. Jez took a swig from his water bottle, got his stuff out of the bag and went over to join Finn. 'Right, Finn, I'm going to thrash you today', he said with a wicked grin. 'Don't be too sure, mate', replied Finn. They took up their positions at either end. Finn served first and Jez returned the ball with a very fast back hand.

What sport are Finn and Jez playing? How do you know? What clues tell you so?

Part 1 - Categories

Story 2

Gerry Burton sighed. 'I'm sorry Mrs Spencer but it's not good news. I'm afraid it's completely had it, the compressor's gone and it's really not worth repairing.' Robyn Spencer looked glum as Gerry packed up his tools and left. There was nothing for it; she'd have to get another one today, especially as the weather was so hot. She set off for the nearest showroom. There were all kinds of different models and it was hard to choose. In the end, she chose one with a built-in ice maker. Luckily, it fitted in the back of the car so she could take it straight home.

What was Robyn buying? How do you know? What clues tell you so?

Story 3

Nelly went out to the back and started to go through the bin liners she'd discovered on the front step when she opened up earlier. The first bag was full of really tatty stuff she knew wouldn't sell. This was put into the recycling sack, awaiting collection. Her face brightened up when she opened the second bag, though. 'Wow!', she thought. 'Some of this is really nice! In fact, I'll try that one myself later.' She set to work putting them in various piles. The winter pile would have to be stored until the weather got colder, but some of these summer ones were lovely. She hung them on hangers waiting to be priced. She particularly liked a long floaty one and decided to put it in the window.

What is Nelly sorting? How do you know? What clues tell you so?

Reading Between the Lines Set Two

Story 4

Early April. A chilly morning but with the promise of sunshine later. Dennis went into the shed and fetched what he needed. He laid it all out neatly on the garden table. First, he lined up the trays, then the pots. He found some labels and a pencil. Then, he got the box of packets and sorted them. He filled the trays and pots with compost and used the pencil to mark lines in the trays. He used the same pencil to make holes, three to a pot, for the bigger ones. Then he started opening the packets. After sprinkling and placing and covering, he gave them all a light watering before putting them in the greenhouse to germinate.

What is Dennis dealing with? How do you know? What clues tell you so?

Story 5

Harper was so excited. It was her eighth birthday and when she got up in the morning it felt like magic! She crept downstairs and there, across the doorway, was a banner that said 'Happy 8th Birthday, Harper!' Everyone else was still asleep so Harper crept into the sitting room. There was a pile of presents in the corner. One was a large box, wrapped in Bratz paper. Harper stood there for a moment and swore she heard a rustle in the box. Just then her Dad appeared in the doorway. 'I think you should maybe open that one, Harps', he said. She tore off the paper and looked in amazement at what she saw. Pale grey, long floppy ears, cute whiskers and a little fluffy tail.

What kind of creature was in the box? How do you know? What clues tell you so?

Part 1 - Categories

Story 6

Laura hated this time of year. The weather was lovely so the family wanted to have breakfast in the garden but they always had to come in or get stung. Sometimes, Laura put a jar with a bit of jam in the bottom on the outside window sill. She'd fill it with water and watch while they came and greedily looked for the sugar before getting drowned in the water. She felt a bit mean about this but it was better than the children getting horrid stings. This year was even worse. Jed, who was four, had found a nest of them in the old stable at the back. 'Mum, come and listen to this, it's all buzzing. What's in there?'

What has invaded Laura's garden? How do you know? What clues tell you so?

Level 4

Story 1

Brooklyn loved it when Auntie Flo let her look in the special box on her dressing table. There were hundreds of pairs. Exotic dangly ones, neat little studs in a range of colours, pearl ones and the ones she wore for special occasions. These were kept in their own boxes. Brooklyn couldn't wait till she was old enough to wear them herself.

What does Auntie Flo keep in her special box? How do you know? What clues tell you so?

Reading Between the Lines Set Two

Story 2

They had been Alfie's favourite toys when he was little. At the age of three, he could name all the different species, even the ones with really long names. He knew which were carnivores and which were herbivores and he could tell you how long ago they became extinct.

What were Alfie's favourite toys when he was little? How do you know? What clues tell you so?

Story 3

'Come on Nelson, I'll give you a game', said Gramps reaching in the cupboard for the wooden box. Nelson loved setting the smooth wooden pieces out on the board. 'Who's going to be black today, then?', said Gramps, placing the Black Queen in position.

What kind of game are Nelson and Gramps going to play? How do you know? What clues tell you so?

Story 4

When they'd finished the game, Nelson followed Gramps into the garden. Gramps handed a garden fork to Nelson. 'I reckon they're ready to dig', he said, pointing to some leafy plants. And these need picking today too.' 'What are those?', said Nelson pointing to some small plants with feathery leaves. 'Pull them up and see!', laughed Gramps. By the time they'd finished there was enough for a meal.

What kind of things does Gramps grow in his garden? How do you know? What clues tell you so?

Part 1 – Categories

Story 5

This was Winston's favourite part of the garden centre. He could stand for ages watching them. There were brightly coloured ones and strange greyish brown ones that stayed on the bottom. There was one that looked as if it had wings, gliding majestically through the weeds and the pretend shipwreck.

What does Winston like watching? How do you know? What clues tell you so?

Story 6

Miss Briggs stood in front of the class. 'Look at your worksheets. I want you to shade them as follows: those with four sides blue, three sides yellow, two sides red. Leave those with no sides plain. Then you need to cut them out and stick them in your books.'

What do the class have to shade in and cut out? How do you know? What clues tell you so?

Story 7

Constance walked into the charity shop. She was glad to see there were several on the shelf today. What she really liked was a nice photo of a country cottage or maybe a seaside view with a harbour and boats. The nicest one was Padstow Harbour but it had 1000 pieces which was a bit much. In the end she chose a 500-piece one of a thatched cottage.

What sort of thing is Constance buying? How do you know? What clues tell you so?

Reading Between the Lines Set Two

Story 8

It was an amazing park. There were so many different kinds. The tall, dark evergreens. The ancient ones that children loved to climb. In one area, there were some very young ones, their trunks slim enough to get your hand round. Last month, there had been a storm and one had blown down, blocking the path.

What grows in the park? How do you know? What clues tell you so?

Story 9

'Why have you got so many different sorts, Nana?', asked Layla. 'Well, these big ones are for fabric. Those are the kitchen ones and the green ones are for paper. Then there are the tiny ones in my sewing basket for when I'm doing embroidery. And the little ones in the bathroom are for your nails.'

What is Layla asking about? How do you know? What clues tell you so?

Story 10

Millie must have tried on at least 10 before she made her mind up. She was going to a wedding at the weekend and needed some that would match her outfit. In the end, she went back to the first shop and decided to get the cream ones. They weren't too high and they would go with lots of her clothes.

What sort of thing is Millie buying? How do you know? What clues tell you so?

Part 1 - Categories

Story 11

Old Desmond Curtis had hundreds. He'd been collecting them for years. They were carefully grouped into different subjects so he could always find what he was looking for. Wooden shelves lined his sitting room and hallway. In the kitchen, he had a special shelf for the cookery section.

What did Desmond collect? How do you know? What clues tell you so?

Story 12

It started when Ellie went to Cornwall on holiday. The first one was like a little house, made of shells. After that, whenever she went somewhere with a souvenir shop she'd look for another one. She had pirates, fruit, animals, an ice cream, country cottages and a bright green parrot. The fridge was literally covered in them.

What does Ellie collect? How do you know? What clues tell you so?

Character

Level 1	89
Level 2	93
Level 3	96
Level 4	99

Part 1 - Character

Level 1

Spot the clues that tell you WHAT KIND OF PERSON THE STORY IS ABOUT.

Clues might be about:

- What the person or animal was like
- What sort of things they did
- How people felt about them

Here is an example. The clues are in bold type.

Mandy's **Mum was getting better after a long illness**, but she was still in a wheelchair and there were **lots of things she couldn't yet manage to do**. She always said that she was lucky having Mandy **for her daughter. Every day, Mandy got breakfast** for herself and her two little brothers and **saw them off to their bus for school.** Then she would **do little jobs for her Mum**, clear up the kitchen, and make the boys' beds. After school, she would **get the tea** and settle Jake and Stevie in front of the telly while she did her homework. Their Dad worked long hours and usually got home late, so Mandy's **day often included feeding the cat** and **stuffing the washing machine** with the boys' grubby football clothes. She did often find herself longing for the day when Mum was fit again.

What kind of person is Mandy? How do you know? What clues tell you so?

- *Mandy's mum had been ill and there were lots of jobs she still couldn't manage*
- *Mandy used to get breakfast for her brothers and see them off to school*
- *Then she would do jobs for her Mum*
- *She often fed the cat and loaded the washing machine*

    = She must have been a very kind girl, as she did so many things for her Mum

Other words to describe her might be helpful, considerate.

Reading Between the Lines Set Two

Story 1

The children in Tommy's street always **tried not to go too near Number 14**. There was a notice on its **gate saying 'PRIVATE'** and another one saying '**NO PARKING**'. The postman said there was still another one on the front door saying 'NO JUNK MAIL'. Nobody ever kicked a ball around down that end of the street. Once, a ball had accidentally gone over the fence into Number 14's garden. **Mr. Snodgrass** had come storming out of the house, **threatening the boys with the police**. They never got their ball back. **Mr Snodgrass complained about his neighbours' cat**, **their dog**, the height they cut their hedges and the **noise he could hear from their TV**. At least one lot of neighbours had moved away, unable to bear the atmosphere. Dad said Mr Snodgrass would probably only ever be satisfied if he had emptied the whole street and had it to himself.

What sort of person is Mr Snodgrass? How do you know? What clues tell you so?

What other words would describe him, do you think?

Story 2

The Green family had gone to **the Dogs' Rescue Home** to choose a new dog. There were dogs of every possible shape and size and colour. The children hated the idea of leaving any of them behind. Some of the dogs bounded up, barking excitedly. Some crept up timidly, not sure of their welcome. Some ran around hysterically, falling over their paws. Some just stayed in a corner, looking anxious. **One fat little chap**, not much more than a puppy, ran up to them and then **rolled over on his back** to have his tummy tickled and **waved his paws in the air**. 'I like the look of this little fellow', Dad said as he picked him up. The puppy wriggled with pleasure and licked Dad's face energetically.

What sort of dog was Dad taking a fancy to? How do you know?
What clues tell you so?

Part 1 - Character

Story 3

The new boy was called Callum. Everyone soon found out that, if you were sitting next to Callum, **you could expect to be pinched and poked** and **have your pencils or rubbers nicked**. If the class got up to some mischief, you could be sure Callum would tell on you. Even worse, **he would help himself to things out of your lunchbox** when you weren't looking. If you complained, Callum always made you pay for it somehow. One day, he went too far. The class were running relay races out in the field and **Callum stuck his foot out as Jamie was sprinting off**. Jamie tripped and fell awkwardly. His broken ankle was in plaster for weeks and this time Callum was in serious trouble. He was kept in after school every day for a week.

What sort of boy was Callum? How do you know? What clues tell you so?

What other words would describe him, do you think?

Story 4

The Team 1 chefs in the competition had made a basket out of spun sugar. When it was finished, it looked wonderful, but **delicate as a spider's web**. Someone had to take it in to show to the judges and **Ivan was the obvious choice** for the job. The slightest bump or bang could shatter the basket. It had been built on a base of baking paper, so Ivan got a large tray and **slid the baking paper gently on to it**. He **placed a trolley next to the table** and eased the tray on to the trolley. Now he had to wheel it into the next room, **avoiding any bumps into walls or doors**. Everyone held their breath as Ivan walked carefully to the judges' table safely and gently lifted the precious basket out.

What sort of worker was Ivan? How do you know? What clues tell you so?

What other words would describe him, do you think?

Copyright material from Catherine Delamain & Jill Spring (2018),
Reading Between the Lines Set Two, Routledge

Reading Between the Lines Set Two

Story 5

Mr Singh who kept the 8 till Late Shop was everybody's friend. Stray cats were fed at the backdoor of the shop, while **any visiting dog was always given a little treat** – Mr Singh kept a bag of tiny dog biscuits behind his counter. **Children could be sure of getting a sweet** out of Mr Singh's bowl – sometimes a toffee, sometimes a jelly baby. If it happened to be your birthday, there would be a lollipop or an ice-cream. People raising money for good causes knew that they **would always get a good contribution from Mr Singh**. The local primary school had recently had a lot of beautiful new equipment for the playground and the rumour was that Mr Singh was largely responsible. Mrs Singh was hugely proud of him, although she teased him that he gave so much away there would soon be nothing left for his family to live on!

What sort of man was Mr Singh? How do you know? What clues tell you so?

There are two good words to choose to describe him. What other words would describe him, do you think?

Story 6

Ava had been away at an activity park for the weekend and **she had won a singing competition**. On Monday morning, Ava made sure that everybody knew about it. She **kept the certificate in her pocket** and brought it out **to show all the teachers**. She told the music teacher that she didn't want to be in the choir any more, as **she was a better standard than they were**. Next day, she brought in a newspaper that had an article about Zog, the singer who had judged her competition and asked Miss Anderson to pin it up on the board. '**Zog was really nice**', she told everyone. 'He said **I showed real promise. He said I had a very mature voice for my age**.' Her friends got fed up with her and told her to change the record, but there was no stopping Ava.

What sort of person was Ava? How do you know? What clues tell you so?

What other words would describe her, do you think?

Part 1 - Character

Level 2

Story 1

The other boys were already practising at the nets when Finley arrived at the field. His friend Oscar had cried off at the last minute with a bad cold and Finley was **braving a whole team of unknown boys on his own**. He stood on the sidelines watching, **feeling shy and rather unhappy**. Then a tall boy spotted him and ran up. 'Hi', he said, 'You must be Finley. I'm Freddie, captain for today. **Come and meet the gang**.' They walked over to the nets. The boy who was bowling pocketed the ball and the batsman put down his bat. Soon the **whole team were gathered round Finley, grinning and telling him their names**. 'Are you any good at wicket keeping?', asked one of them, and when Finley said 'Not bad', he said '**Come on, then, I'll help you find some pads**'. By the time they stopped practising for tea, Finley felt as if he'd known the boys all his life.

What sort of boys did Finley join to play cricket? How do you know? What clues tell you so?

Story 2

Freya had two little brothers aged two and four and a sister called Poppy, just a bit younger than Freya. The boys kept their mum very busy and **both the girls had jobs to do to help out**. Freya's jobs were to take the dog for a short walk after school and to supervise the boys putting their toys away before bedtime. **Poppy's were to feed the budgie** and **clean out his cage once a week**. Freya was **sick of having to do Poppy's jobs for her**. Mum **knew what Poppy was like**, though. 'I'm going to give her a different job', she told Freya. 'And she's going to lose pocket money if she doesn't do it. But I **expect I shall end up doing it myself** – or it might not get done this year, or next year – or ever! I'm so glad I can depend on you, Freya.'

What word might describe Poppy? How do you know? What clues tell you so?

What other words that mean the same sort of thing would describe her, do you think?

Reading Between the Lines Set Two

Story 3

When the Simpsons moved in to their new house, they soon discovered something about the old lady next door. She seemed to **spend all her time at one of the windows**, often with her **eyes to a pair of binoculars**. If the children were in the back garden, the old lady usually appeared at a back bedroom window. If anything was going on round the front, there the old lady was, this time **peering out of her sitting room window**. Sometimes, she would come into her own garden and lean over the fence. She **always had a string of questions**. 'Who was it they had staying with them? Was that the ambulance at Number 7 this morning? Do you know what's wrong?' The children enjoyed thinking up weird things to do in the garden to puzzle the poor old lady, but Mum said not to tease her – she was lonely and had nothing else to do.

What sort of old lady lived next door to the Simpsons? How do you know? What clues tell you so?

What other words that mean the same sort of thing would describe her, do you think?

Story 4

The twins got to the station with about three minutes to spare and then had trouble with the ticket machine. They reached the platform to see their train just pulling out and a guard stopped them from trying to jump on while it was moving. **Chloe burst into tears**. **'Whatever are we going to do?', she sobbed**. 'Dad will be waiting for us and won't know what's happened and we'll miss the match and I need to go to the toilet!' **Leo handed her his hankie**. '**Don't get in a flap**', he said. 'First things first. The toilet is over there. I'll wait for you here. While you're in there, **I'll phone Dad** on his mobile and tell him **we'll be on the next train**. Then we'll find out what time it goes. See? **Nothing to it!**'

What sort of boy is Leo? How do you know? What clues tell you so?

Is Chloe like Leo, do you think?

Part 1 - Character

Story 5

The rubber dinghy with the two small children in it had been floating in the shallow water near the pier. The wind began to freshen and the sea was getting wavy. It only took a few minutes for the **little boat to drift out towards the end of the pier** and the children clearly had no idea how to paddle their tiny craft. It **began to spin** and the **bigger waves started to toss it about**. It was **now in deep water**. People on the beach who saw what was happening watched in alarm. Some of the men began to strip off and run down to the edge of the sea, but before anyone could reach the water, **a figure** appeared **on the pier. Dropping his jacket and kicking off his shoes**, he **did a perfect dive**, surfacing **a few yards from the bobbing boat**. He swam back to the beach pushing the dinghy in front of him, with two frightened children holding tight to the sides.

What sort of man rescued the children? How do you know? What clues tell you so?

WHat other words would describe him, do you think?

Story 6

The trailers were finished and the **main film began**, with **creepy music** playing. A vast jungle appeared on the screen. Between the twisted trunks of the trees you could catch glimpses of a **shadowy figure** that looked something like a dog, and following it **were men with guns**. Now and then they seemed to be catching up with it, but then again it would disappear into the gloom. The scene cut to the battlements of a castle, where a **hideous figure – half man, half wolf** – was prowling. It was at this point that **Isla got under her seat** and **pulled her jumper over her head. Nothing could persuade her to come out**, so in the end the whole family decided to give up and go home. Isla was in tears. 'I thought it was a nature film about animals', she sobbed. It took a takeaway fish and chips supper and a quiet hour of Mary Poppins on the TV before Isla was calm again.

What sort of girl was Isla? How do you know? What clues tell you so?

Copyright material from Catherine Delamain & Jill Spring (2018),
Reading Between the Lines Set Two, Routledge

Reading Between the Lines Set Two

Level 3

In the next stories, you have to *find the clues yourself.*

Story 1

Ethan didn't enjoy having tea with his godmother. For one thing, he could never think what to talk to her about and for another she always had a kind of cake he hated. But the worst thing was she made him feel so uncomfortable. He tried to explain to his Mum. 'If you stand up, she goes and plumps up the cushion where you have been sitting. If you drop a tiny crumb on the carpet, she dashes off to find a brush and dustpan. I'm always scared I'll knock a whole mug over or squash a biscuit on the carpet.' Mum just laughed. 'You can tell she's never had children of her own', she reminded him.

Can you think of a word that describes Ethan's godmother? How do you know? What clues tell you so?

What other words would describe her, do you think?

Story 2

Muhammad and his family lived on the fifth floor and in the flat opposite lived the oldest man Muhammad had ever seen. He was so small and wizened he looked as if a puff of wind would blow him away. Muhammad often carried his bag for him when they met. The day the lift broke down, Muhammad thought about their old neighbour. 'He goes out most days', he said. 'And there's no way he can manage the stairs. I'll go and see if I can fetch anything for him.' He ended up with quite a long shopping list. The old man grinned as he gave it to Muhammad. 'I'm not going to waste the chance of having a porter', he chuckled.

What sort of boy was Muhammad? How do you know? What clues tell you so?

Part 1 – Character

Story 3

Amelia was well-known among her friends for never having what she needed with her. They were used to having to lend her a rubber, a biro, a notebook, a copy of the week's lesson timetable. When she didn't turn up in time for a lesson, they used to make a guess as to where she would be and someone would go and find her before the teacher noticed her absence. However, sometimes there was nothing they could do to rescue her. The visit to the swimming pool was Amelia's downfall. She turned up with a towel and goggles, but no swimming costume. Her friends could only feel sorry for her, as she sat in one of the seats for spectators and watched the races from the side.

What word could describe Amelia? How do you know? What clues tell you so?

What other words would describe her, do you think?

Story 4

Everyone in Year 10, especially the girls, admired Freddie. It wasn't just that he was so tall and good looking, but he was brilliant at every sport. He regularly won matches at tennis and swimming and was in the first team for football and cricket. He always made light of his successes. 'It wasn't much', he would say. 'George would have passed me if we'd had another two metres to go.' If it was a football win, he would praise the other members of the team and say the success was mainly due to them. When you praised Freddie to his face he looked very embarrassed, went red and changed the subject as quickly as he could.

What sort of boy was Freddie? How do you know? What clues tell you so?

Reading Between the Lines Set Two

Story 5

The magistrate pushed his glasses up on his nose and looked sternly at the accused teenager. Then he looked at the document in front of him. 'This is an extraordinarily long list of offences for someone so young', he said. 'There are five counts of shoplifting, six of petty theft from private houses, three of picking pockets and several of travelling on buses or trains without a ticket. You have also consistently lied to the police about your whereabouts when questioned. Have you anything to say for yourself?' The man in the dock looked mulish and muttered: 'Not guilty.'

What sort of man was the magistrate talking to? How do you know? What clues tell you so?

Story 6

Mum said maybe it was the wonderful smell of fresh bread and croissants in her bakery that did the trick. Mrs Honeybun was always smiling and a chat with her could brighten up the gloomiest day. 'Always look on the bright side', was her favourite saying and that was exactly what she did. If it rained, she said it would be good for the gardens. When her van broke down, she said it would be good for her delivery boy to do a bit of walking for a change. She was even smiling the morning she found a leaky pipe in her back room and water all over the floor. 'Could have been worse', she said.

What sort of person was Mrs Honeybun? How do you know? What clues tell you so?

Part 1 - Character

Level 4

Story 1

There was a little posy of garden flowers on the doorstep on Mum's birthday. 'That's the dear woman next door', said Mum. 'She always remembers.'

What sort of person was the woman next door? How do you know? What clues tell you so?

Story 2

Joshua was ordering his foreign currency. 'Goodness, where is it this time?', asked the man in the bank, who knew Josh. 'Backpacking in Thailand', said Joshua. 'On my own for a change.'

What sort of boy was Joshua? Had he been travelling before? How do you know? What clues tell you so?

Does he always go on his own?

Story 3

Aidan was full of his latest idea for getting rich. He was going to grow all sorts of shrubs in pots and hire them out for marquees for parties and weddings. Never mind that he had no money, only a tiny garden and no van. And there was a big garden centre just down the road doing the same thing.

What sort of man was Aidan? How do you know? What clues tell you so?

Has he made plans for getting rich before? Might some of the words used to describe him be good qualities and some not so good, do you think?

Reading Between the Lines Set Two

Story 4

Florence was full of rosy plans ideas for her future, although she was only eight. Sometimes, the idea was a top vet, sometimes, a brain surgeon, sometimes, a famous film star. 'Prime minister next, I expect', Mum used to joke.

What sort of girl was Florence? How do you know? What clues tell you so?

Story 5

Jim the plumber was liable to arrive while you were still having breakfast and he rarely got home before seven or eight. His wife joked that she saw more of her Granny in Scotland than she did of Jim.

What sort of man was Jim? How do you know? What clues tell you so?

What other words would to describe him, do you think?

Story 6

Sophie and Olivia were halfway down the street by the time Olivia had sorted out her change. 'They've given me too much', she said. '£1.50 too much, to be exact. I must go back.' 'I shouldn't bother', Sophie said. 'It's no big deal.' 'Sorry, I must', Olivia said, and set off briskly back to the shop.

What sort of person is Olivia? How do you know? What clues tell you so?

Was Sophie like her?

Story 7

Rohan had taken to hanging out with a new crowd of friends and Mrs Puri didn't like the look of them at all. She didn't approve of their long hair, their weird clothes or their raucous music. Mr Puri told her to relax. 'There's no harm in them', he said. 'Give them a year or so and they'll grow up.'

What sort of man is Mr Puri? How do you know? What clues tell you so?

And what about Mrs Puri?

Story 8

Nina felt pretty much ready for her new job. She thought that after the last two hard years, she should be able to cope with this one, even though it meant a lot more responsibility. The interviews had gone really well. Nina was looking forward to Monday.

What sort of person is Nina? How do you know? What clues tell you so?

Story 9

It turned out to be a lovely day for the fete. Lots of people came and the celebrity arrived on time to open the proceedings. 'So much for Ben's rotten forecast', thought Simon, 'No sign of rain, and a good crowd. I bet we'll make even more than last year, whatever he may think.'

What sort of person is Ben? How do you know? What clues tell you so?

Reading Between the Lines Set Two

Story 10

Celina had no brothers or sisters, but she had a host of friends who nobody else could see. She talked to them in the long grassy area in the park, out in the woods on walks, up in her bedroom. She could tell you exactly what they all looked like. Her favourite was a fairy by the name of Bluebell.

What sort of child was Celina? How do you know? What clues tell you so?

Story 11

Alvita had spent her pocket money on a huge bag of mixed sweets. Little Shona looked on longingly as Alvita slowly popped one sweet after another into her mouth and made 'yum-yum' noises. Shona had shared hers with Alvita yesterday, but it didn't look as if her sister was going to pay her back.

What sort of girl was Alvita? How do you know? What clues tell you so?

Was Shona like her or not, do you think?

Story 12

Mum found living next door to Mrs Fowler quite a strain. If she were hanging up her washing, Mrs Fowler would lean over the hedge and suggest a better brand of washing powder. If she were gardening, Mrs Fowler always knew it was too cold for sowing seeds. Mum said she would have to do her outside jobs by night with a torch!

What sort of person was Mrs. Fowler? How do you know? What clues tell you so?

Emotion

Level 1   104

Level 2   107

Level 3   110

Level 4   112

Level 1

Spot the clues that tell you *HOW PEOPLE ARE FEELING*.

Clues might be about:

- What a person felt like – happy, sad, scared
- How a creature might be feeling
- How groups of people were feeling, would be feeling

Here is an example. The clues are in bold type.

The first day of the family **holiday** had arrived. Katy jumped out of bed and ran to the window. It looked like a **gorgeous morning**, the sun was out, the sky was blue and every bird in the world seemed to be chirping and twittering. Katy went to the cupboard and started digging out some of the **stuff** she would want **for the beach** – swimming things, flip flops, and sunhat. She thought of seven whole days with **no school** and **Mum and Dad off work** as well. Dad was fun to have at the seaside, he always thought of great things for them to do and maybe this year he would teach her how to use a mask and snorkel and flippers. Katy's **best friend, Lily, was coming with them, too.**

What is Katy feeling like? How do you know? What clues tell you so?

- *They were going on holiday*
- *It was a gorgeous morning*
- *They were going to the beach*
- *Mum and Dad were off work*
- *Katy's best friend was coming with them*

    = Katy must have been feeling happy

Part 1 - Emotion

Story 1

Jo remembered just as he got off the school bus. He had been in a rush that morning and although he had chucked some lettuce and carrots at Perkin, his rabbit, he **hadn't cleaned his cage** or given him fresh water. Dad met him at the front door with a **face like thunder**. 'You begged and begged for that rabbit', he said the minute Jo stepped into the house. 'You promised faithfully you would look after him. This is the third time your Mum or I have had to do your job for you. That rabbit is your responsibility, and **if this happens one more time Perkin will go** to someone who will care for him properly.'

How was Jo's Dad feeling? How do you know? What clues tell you so?

What other words would describe him, do you think?

Story 2

Bastian thought the drizzly grey **weather looked the way he felt**. It was the first day he had to **go to school without his friend**, Mohammed, who had moved to live somewhere called Bootle, miles away. They would probably **never be able to get together again**. What was he going to do without him? **Mo had made all the difference at school** and they had often spent their evenings together, either at Bastian's house or at Mo's. Mo's mum made smashing cakes and biscuits, too. At the weekend, the two of them always had things to do together, even if it was only kicking a ball around on the football pitch. He wondered what Mo would be doing today.

How was Bastian feeling? How do you know? What clues tell you so?

Reading Between the Lines Set Two

Story 3

The **theatre was packed**. Five or 600 teenagers filled every seat and there was a **terrific buzz of conversation**. Adele was the star attraction and **Arjun and Aaron could hardly wait**. They had been so lucky to get tickets. Arjun looked at his watch. '**Three minutes to go**', he said. As the minutes ticked by, the noise of the chatter grew louder and then at last the **lights in the auditorium dimmed**, the curtains drew back and the audience fell silent. The boys held their breath. Now, **at last, Adele would come on to the stage**.

How was the crowd in the theatre feeling? How do you know? What clues tell you so?

Story 4

Anna was so excited. Her friend **Daisy was coming to stay for the whole weekend**. Daisy's family had moved away and **they hadn't seen one another for the whole half-term**. When they lived nearby, Daisy often came for sleepovers or Anna went to Daisy's house. It had been almost as good as having a sister. **Daisy was coming on the train** on her own and **Anna and her Dad were going to meet her** at the station. Just then came the phone call to say Daisy was not very well and wouldn't be coming after all. How quickly everything could change.

How did Anna feel when she heard that Daisy would not be coming?
How do you know? What clues tell you so?

Story 5

Jack had a little gang. Everyone knew about it, even the teachers at school, but the gang hardly ever got caught. That morning, Lucy was on her way to her friend's house when she saw **Jack's gang hanging around** outside Mr Patel's paper shop. Lucy **saw the boys wander** casually up **to the shop**, look around at the door and windows, put their heads together and then move off. '**Now what are they planning?**', Lucy wondered. She was really fond of Mr Patel.

How did Lucy feel when she saw the gang outside Mr Patel's shop?
How do you know? What clues tell you so?

Copyright material from Catherine Delamain & Jill Spring (2018),
Reading Between the Lines Set Two, Routledge

Part 1 - Emotion

Story 6

It was Sunday morning and Jayden was in the middle of his newspaper round. Next on the list was Mr Wentworth. **Three enormous dogs lived here** and Jayden always tried to time his visit when the dogs were safely inside. All clear today. Jayden opened the gate and as he started up the path the front door flew open and **the dogs came hurtling towards him**, barking madly. Too late to run! Jayden stood still, **heart pounding**. Mr Wentworth came to the door shouting: 'Here dogs, come here! Don't worry, Jayden, they're all big softies.' The dogs slowed down and stopped barking. Mr Wentworth introduced them to Jayden, who got wet licks all over his hands.

How did Jayden feel when the dogs started rushing towards him? How do you know? What clues tell you so?

Level 2

Story 1

The postman rang the doorbell and handed over **a parcel addressed to Tia**. She **didn't recognize the writing** on the outside and when she asked her Mum, Mum didn't recognise it either. 'Funny', said Tia, 'It **isn't my birthday** or anything. What can it be?' 'Only one way to find out', said Mum. 'Better try opening it!' Tia unwrapped the paper and found a pretty box inside. Inside the box, nestling in cotton wool, was a gorgeous charm bracelet made of silver. Tia hunted through the cotton wool but there was no letter or note. Tia thought perhaps a letter or a phone call would follow, but the weeks passed and she was still **no nearer an answer**.

How did Tia feel about her parcel? How do you know? What clues tell you so?

Reading Between the Lines Set Two

Story 2

The **school was keeping bees**. Two beekeepers had come with three hives and installed them at the bottom of the big field. Now Year 5 pupils were being dressed up in special hats and suits to protect them from stings and they were **opening up the hives to see the honey**. The beekeepers showed them how to find the Queen Bee and they put a mark on her so they would be able to find her easily another time. Then they all had a turn at scraping off some of the honey into a dish and tasting it. **Billy usually spent his time in lessons daydreaming** about riding his bike or going fishing with his uncle. But this business with **the bees was a different matter** and he **couldn't wait for the next visit** to the beehives.

How did Billy feel about the bees and learning how to look after them? How do you know? What clues tell you so?

Story 3

Emily had really tried her absolute best over the English homework. She **liked Miss Collins** and **wanted so much to impress her**. She wrote out her answers on scrap paper and then copied them carefully into her exercise book. She checked her spellings on her laptop and put them all right. In class next day, she took her book up to Miss Collins and waited nervously for what she would say. **Miss Collins looked through the homework carefully** and then she looked at Emily and **gave her a beaming smile**.

How did Miss Collins feel about Emily and her homework? How do you know? What clues tell you so?

Part 1 - Emotion

Story 4

Some **new people had moved in next door**. Aneena and her brother were hoping there would be some children for them to play with. All day masses of stuff was being carried into the house from the removal van – beds, chairs, lamps, fridges, boxes of books – but it was hard to tell whether there were any toys. There were no bikes, anyway. **At the end of a whole week they hadn't seen anybody go into** or come out of **the house**, although **lights went on at night** and the milkman and postman were calling. **Aneena decided to keep watch on Saturday** and she took turns with Ashok.

How did Aneena feel about the house next door? How do you know? What clues tell you so?

Story 5

Jock and his family had moved down to Yorkshire from Scotland. In Scotland, **they had lived in a little town where everybody seemed to know everybody else** and, in the evenings, **three or four boys would always get together** and kick a ball around or just hang out and chat. Now the family was **living** in a farmhouse out **in the middle of nowhere**. It was a beautiful place and Mum and Dad were busy and happy with the animals and all the jobs, but Jock couldn't help wishing they were back in their old house. He began to think **how he could get into the nearest village** and see if he could **find some friends**.

How was Jock feeling in the new house? How do you know? What clues tell you so?

Reading Between the Lines Set Two

Story 6

Joshua was in the school library. They were supposed to **take one book home every weekend** and tell the class about it the next week. Joshua was feeling so miserable and fed up he couldn't work up any interest in reading. Then he **suddenly saw a book** that seemed to be made for him. It was called *My Horrid Baby Sister*. He flicked over some pages. Yes, there were all the aunts and uncles and **neighbours cooing over the crib.** There was the mother feeding the baby while the **big boy was dying for his tea**. There was the **pile of presents left for a baby who couldn't even sit up yet**, let alone do anything interesting. This was a book Joshua really wanted to read!

**What does Joshua feel about his new baby sister? How do you know?
What clues tell you so?**

Level 3

In the next stories, *find the clues yourself.*

Story 1

Grandma was pottering about, taking forever to get her coat on and find her handbag. The taxi was already waiting outside and it had been there for ages. At long last she was ready, coat and hat on, umbrella and handbag over her arm. Grandpa whistled through his teeth when they got into the taxi and he looked at the meter.

**How was Grandpa feeling as they got into the taxi? How do you know?
What clues tell you so?**

Part 1 - Emotion

Story 2

Anika couldn't keep her mind on her lessons that morning. She was remembering her little hamster, usually so lively and responsive, lying curled up in his bedding and not wanting anything to eat. Anika had taken him to the vet the day before and he had just said to keep Treacle warm and make sure he had plenty of water. Anika looked at her watch. She would be home in three quarters of an hour.

How is Anika feeling? How do you know? What clues tell you so?

Story 3

Oliver had been carrying his secret round with him for days. What had made him keep that wallet he'd found in the playground, instead of handing it in to a teacher? With every day that passed, it became more impossible to confess. When the class teacher looked round the room and asked if anyone knew anything about it, Oliver felt sick. When Mr Jones started to question them one at a time, Oliver wished the ground would open and swallow him up.

How did Oliver feel when the teacher questioned them about the theft? How do you know? What clues tell you so?

Story 4

Ben was going on a plane journey on his own for the first time. He had told Dad he wanted to do it entirely by himself except for being dropped off at the airport. His godfather was going to meet him in San Francisco. But now the array of check-in machines, check-in counters, departure boards and swirling crowds was a bit daunting. Dad had assured him that the airline people wouldn't let him get on the wrong plane, but it didn't seem quite so easy somehow now the moment had come.

How did Ben feel at the airport? How do you know? What clues tell you so?

Reading Between the Lines Set Two

Story 5

Kiara and Myra had had a tremendous row. It had ended up with them both shouting that they didn't want to be friends any more, that she would never come to the other's house again and that they wouldn't ask one another to their birthday parties. Myra had burst into tears and run off into her house and Kiara had stumped off home, still feeling furious. Now she was remembering all the good times she and Myra had had together, how much they had shared and how they had planned all sorts of exciting things for the summer holidays. She knew she had really upset Myra and began to go over all the horrible things she had said to her.

How is Kiara feeling about what she had said to Myra? How do you know? What clues tell you so?

Story 6

Mr Blake sat down in his favourite chair. Almost at once he got up and straightened some books on the shelf. Then he sat down again. Then he got up and tidied the magazines on the table. He thought of making a cup of tea, but he didn't really want one. He looked out of the window and thought he ought to cut the creeper back – later. Why wouldn't that wretched phone ring? It was already after six.

What sort of state do you think Mr. Blake was in? How do you know? What clues tell you so?

Level 4

Story 1

Adnan pulled off his heavy work gloves and kicked off his wellingtons in the shed. It simply wasn't fair. He had worked all day for Farmer King and he'd only been paid the same as the others who started at lunchtime.

How was Adnan feeling? How do you know? What clues tell you so?

Part 1 - Emotion

Story 2

Marisha stood up as tall as she could and walked steadily on to the stage. The judge placed the cardboard crown carefully on to Marisha's head and there was a storm of clapping. As she left the stage, Marisha caught sight of her mother in the audience, wiping away a tear.

How was Marisha feeling? What makes you think so? What clues tell you so?

Story 3

Jake felt in his pocket for his ticket. Not there! He felt in the other pocket – it was empty. Just as Jake was beginning to wonder desperately what he was going to do, a girl ran up to him. 'I think you dropped this', she said, handing Jake his ticket.

How did Jake feel when the girl gave him his lost ticket? How do you know? What clues tell you so?

Story 4

Ed got into the little glider beside the pilot. He had always wanted to do this! 'The plane will tow us up over the mountain into the thermal and cast us off', said the pilot. 'Then I shall hand over to you.' Ed's jaw dropped. This was a bigger step than he'd been expecting.

How did Ed feel when the pilot said he would be taking over the plane? How do you know? What clues tell you so?

Copyright material from Catherine Delamain & Jill Spring (2018),
Reading Between the Lines Set Two, Routledge

Reading Between the Lines Set Two

Story 5

The group had gone in to the maze at Hampton Court. They had been wandering round in it for half an hour, trying to get to the middle, but they kept on finding themselves back at the entrance again. The decided on one more try and this time they could actually see the statue in the central square if they stood on tiptoe, tantalizingly close . . . but they were no nearer to reaching it.

How do you think the people in the maze were feeling? How do you know? What clues tell you so?

What other words would describe them, so you think?

Story 6

Meriel had taken a photo of the pheasant that had strayed into their garden. She had got really close and the result was a super picture, showing all the bird's gorgeous colours. Meriel had posted the photo on Instagram and there had already been 10,000 'likes'! She couldn't wait to tell her friends.

How did Meriel feel when she saw how many 'likes' there had been? How do you know? What clues tell you so?

Story 7

Tess stopped just inside the door. The room was full of people, all talking and laughing together. As far as Tess could see, there was nobody in the room that she knew except Anya, who had invited her. She thought of turning round and going straight home again, but decided to brave it out.

How did Tess feel when she got to the party? How do you know? What clues tell you so?

Part 1 - Emotion

Story 8

The woman stood in her kitchen looking at the disaster. The tap wouldn't turn off and the water had filled the sink and was starting to overflow. She had spread towels on the floor and every bucket, pan and jug was full of water. 'Please let the plumber hurry', she thought

How did the woman feel as the water continued to flood her kitchen? How do you know? What clues tell you so?

Story 9

Aman opened his email inbox nervously and could hardly believe his eyes. Better results than he had dared to hope for! They would get him in to either of his preferred colleges and get him a pat on the back from his tutors too. 'Phew', he thought. 'This is more than I deserved!'

How did Aman feel when he read his email? How do you know? What clues tell you so?

Story 10

Jo had been living alone all winter in the depths of the country, working on his latest book. The weather had been horrible, the book was proving a challenge and Jo had been feeling pretty low. That day a spring sun was shining and a new way to tackle the book had popped into Jo's head.

How was Jo feeling that day? How do you know? What clues tell you so?

Reading Between the Lines Set Two

Story 11

It was all over, all the effort and the worry and the hard work. She had done her best and there was nothing more to be done. Susie lay in the hammock under the trees, her arms trailing over the sides and listened dreamily to the sounds of the birds.

How was Susie feeling as she lay in the hammock? How do you know? What clues tell you so?

Story 12

The soldier kept an eye on the clock as the man in the ticket office laboriously filled in forms, folding each one carefully and putting it into a file. Then he turned away and began to open a filing cabinet. Corporal Evans wanted to scream as the hands ticked round and he heard a train approaching.

How did Corporal Toby Evans feel as he watched the ticket clerk? How do you know? What clues tell you so?

Cause and effect

Level 1   118

Level 2   122

Level 3   125

Level 4   127

Reading Between the Lines Set Two

Level 1

Spot the clues that tell you WHY SOMETHING HAPPENED OR WHY SOMETHING MIGHT BE GOING TO HAPPEN.

Clues may be about:

- Why something happened
- Why something might be going to happen
- What made it happen

Here is an example. The clues are in bold type.

The three sisters stood in the queue for the check-in desk. They were excited about their three day break in Barcelona. Ally put her case on the weigh-in and handed over her passport. Next was Cassie. She lifted the case onto the belt and handed her **passport** to the girl on the desk. 'Excuse me, Madam,' said the girl, looking closely at Cassie. 'The name on this passport is **Chris Parks**; there seems to be a mistake.' Cassie grabbed the passport and gazed in horror. 'Oh no! I picked up ***his* by mistake!**', she hissed at her sisters.

What was Cassie's mistake? How do you know?

- **The name on the passport is wrong**
- **It's her partner's name**

    = She must have picked up his passport by mistake

Part 1 - Cause and effect

Story 1

'Don't forget to put the **white** wash on', called Amy as she left for work. Matt loaded a pile **of white sheets and towel**s into the **washing basket**. At that moment, his phone rang and he spent the next 10 minutes talking to Amy's mother. Meanwhile Eddie, their three-year-old son, found Amy's **red** silk scarf on the floor. The dog had trodden on it with muddy feet and it was covered in paw marks. Eddie decided he would be all grown-up and helpful so he popped the scarf into the **washing machine**. Matt came downstairs carrying the washing basket. 'Come on Matt, get your shoes, we're taking Nana to the shops.' He **loaded the machine** and switched it on and the two of them set off. When they arrived home, they were greeted by a very cross-looking Amy. 'WHAT have you done?', she demanded, pointing at the **wet washing**.

Why was Amy cross? How do you know? What clues tell you so?

Story 2

Gemma put the **quiches on the worktop** to cool down. The next job was to get the tables laid and the drinks sorted out. She looked at her watch – she had about two hours before the **guests** arrived. It was a hot afternoon and **she'd left the kitchen window open**. Gemma was busy in the dining room so she didn't notice the thud as **Rupert landed on the kitchen floor**. Half an hour later she went back into the kitchen and stood, horrified. What on earth had **happened to the quiches**? Then she saw Rupert, sitting in the sun, licking his lips.

What had happened? How do you know? What clues tell you so?

Reading Between the Lines Set Two

Story 3

Maddie was excited and nervous at the same time. Tomorrow, she started work as a junior reporter on the local newspaper. She put her clothes ready, washed her hair and set the alarm on her bedside clock **for 6.30 am**. That should give her **plenty of time** to catch the bus into town. The weather was very warm and during the evening large clouds began to appear. Maddie went to bed early but was woken in the middle of the night by a **clap of thunder** followed by torrential rain. She finally fell into a deep sleep at about three in the morning. In what seemed like about five minutes she was woken by the sound of her neighbour's motorbike as he set off for work. Maddie sat bolt upright. Chas never left for work **before eight o'clock**. She looked in horror at the clock. It said **1.45**!

What do you think had happened? How do you know? What clues tell you so?

Story 4

'The inlaid **box** is yours', said Aunt Wynn to Jan, about three weeks before she died. Now Jan was sorting out the old lady's belongings. Most of it was shabby and drab and she bundled it into a bin liner to take to the charity shop. The inlaid box sat on her kitchen table, unopened because she didn't have a **key**. She looked at it carefully. It was probably over 100 years old and looked good condition. There was something inside because, when Jan shook it, it rattled. However, she couldn't open it and didn't like to break the lock. The next day she took the bin liner to the charity shop. A friendly woman called Hilary took it and thanked her. Later, Hilary opened the bag and started going through the contents. Most of it went straight into the recycling bag but near the bottom Hilary found a little cloth bag with a **key** in it. She took the bag out and put it **somewhere safe**, hoping the lady who'd brought the **bin liner** would come back.

Why did Hilary put the key somewhere safe? Why did Hilary hope the lady would come back? How do you know? What clues tell you so?

Part 1 - Cause and effect

Story 5

Seth liked **science** when it was proper experiments, with chemicals and Bunsen burners and stuff. But he wasn't so keen when it was about **plants and nature**. So while Miss Baxter was giving instructions about what to do, Seth was thinking about the skate park. 'Right, Class 5, let's get started.' Seth nudged his friend Arto. 'What we got to do Art?' Arto was busy putting a bunch of white daisies in a beaker of **blue liquid**. He shrugged at Seth and replied, 'That's what she said.' Luckily, it was the last lesson on a Friday afternoon so Seth just copied what Arto was doing. He was surprised on Monday when he came into class and **all the white daisies had turned blue.**

Why do you think the flowers turned blue? How do you know? What clues tell you so?

Story 6

In July, there was a heatwave for a few days. On Tuesday, Tess went up to the attic and opened the **skylight windows** a little bit, so the air would circulate. Her sister was coming to stay in a couple of days and Tess didn't want it to be hot and stuffy up there. Tess worked in a charity shop on Thursdays and this week it was busy, full of people trying to get in **out of the rain**, which poured down without stopping all day long. When she got home, she noticed a **slight breeze** at the top of the stairs. Weird, because her bedroom window was shut. Then she remembered and ran up to the **attic**.

What had happened in the attic? How do you know? What clues tell you so?

Reading Between the Lines Set Two

Level 2

Story 1

Ben Hodges was very pleased with his new lawn. It made the garden look bigger somehow. Annie, his wife, laughed about it to her friends 'He's obsessed with it – but it's only for looking at, no one's allowed to actually walk on it!' Every morning and night Ben **switched the sprinkler on**, following the advice to keep it well-watered the first summer. Today was Saturday and Ben and Annie were going to a barbecue in the middle of tomorrow afternoon. Ben decided to leave the watering until they came back. It was nearly 11 pm when they finally got back. Ben switched on the **sprinkler**. 'Ben', he heard Annie call. 'Can you come and help me. I've dropped my contact lens.' It took them about half an hour to find the tiny lens, caught on the bathroom curtains. 'Phew, I really thought it had gone', said Annie, as they got ready for bed. Next morning, Ben was horrified to find **a huge puddle of water lapping at the back door**.

What had happened? How do you know? What clues tell you so?

Story 2

Nadya stacked the sixth box of bean bags in the corner of the PE cupboard with a sigh. She could **hear the class in the hall**. Today, they were using the apparatus, which was her **favourite PE lesson**. 'It's just so unfair', she muttered to herself, heaving a pile of mats into the corner. It hadn't been her fault that baby Ravi had been awake all night so that mum had **missed the alarm**. The family were **late** and cross and Nadya didn't have **time to check she had all she needed** for school before she ran for the bus. 'Oh well, I'd better finish this lot. I don't want to have to miss break as well.'

Why is Nadya fed up? How do you know? What clues tell you so?

Part 1 - Cause and effect

Story 3

Ruby and her cousin Lexi were on the beach with Lexi's Mum. It was the first day of their holiday and they'd found buckets, spades and fishing nets in the shed at the holiday cottage. They decided to **make a really big castle** and set to work. First, they made a mound of sand and levelled it so the top was flat. Then, they used the buckets to put four towers on the top. Ruby collected pointed **limpet shells to decorate it** and Lexi dug a moat. The morning went really quickly and soon Lexi's mum said they were **going to the beach café** to get some chips for **lunch**. They sat on a bench in the harbour watching the fishermen unloading their boats. When they'd finished, they walked back toward the beach but by now the **tide was coming in**. 'Where's our castle?' said Ruby. 'I'm sure it was here.' As the wave receded she could see a **little pile of limpet shells** but no sign of a castle.

Why can't the girls find the castle? Why is there a little pile of limpet shells? How do you know? What clues tell you so?

Story 4

Once upon a time there was a boy called Jack who lived in a little cottage with his mother. They were very poor. One day Jack's mother told Jack to take the cow and **sell it** in the market so they would have some money for food. On the way to market, Jack met a strange old man. He persuaded Jack to give him the **cow in exchange for a handful of beans**. Jack wasn't quite sure but, in the end, he agreed. The man went off leading the cow and Jack **walked home with the beans**. Jack's mum was furious when he told her what he'd done. She **flung the beans** out of the window and Jack went to bed with no dinner. When Jack woke the next morning, his room was **strangely dark**. He went over to the window and looked out in astonishment.

Why was Jack's mum furious? Why was Jack's room strangely dark? How do you know? What clues tell you so?

Reading Between the Lines Set Two

Story 5

Mina's Nan had a tame jackdaw. In the summer, when the window was open the bird would fly in and perch on the back of a chair. It had shiny black eyes and blue-black feathers. Mina's Nan called it Jacko. One Saturday afternoon, Mina called in on Nan. She looked fed up. 'What's the matter Nan?', asked Mina. 'I've **lost one of my favourite earrings**, the silver one with a blue stone in the middle. I wore them yesterday and I remember taking them off last night. I always leave them **on the dressing table** by the mirror.' Mina changed the subject. 'How's Jacko, have you seen him today?' 'He came in this morning early but then flew off. I think he's up in that tree at the end of the garden.' Mina went out into the garden and looked for the bird. Then **something shiny caught her eye**, lying on the gravel path. 'Nan', she called. '**Look what I've found!**'

What do you think Mina found? How did it get there? How do you know? What clues tell you so?

Story 6

Dan was very pleased with his new car. It was much sportier looking than the last one and had built in satnav. He'd decided to get the **diesel** model to save on fuel costs. This weekend he was going to visit his parents in Exeter. It would be good to do a nice long drive and see how well it performed. He set off after work on Friday evening, aiming to get there by about eight o'clock. He stopped at the services just before the dual carriageway to get some **petrol** and a bar of chocolate. It was a windy evening and at first Dan thought it was the wind that seemed to be **slowing the car down a bit**. But it gradually **got worse**. 'Uh oh', thought Dan, wondering what on earth could be wrong. Luckily, there was a garage open **and he pulled in**. 'I filled up with **petrol** about five miles back', he explained to the mechanic, 'and it's been going slower and slower ever since.' '**Petrol you said?**', replied the mechanic, shaking his head.

Why do you think the car has a problem? Why is the mechanic shaking his head? How do you know? What clues tell you so?

Part 1 - Cause and effect

Level 3

In the next stories, you have to *find the clues yourself*.

Story 1

Grandma got the ice-cream out of the freezer ready for when the boys arrived. It wasn't long before she heard them banging on the front door. 'Look what we've got Grandma', they shouted as their Mum came in carrying a little puppy. She was a sweet little thing, black with white paws. 'She's not allowed to go outside yet 'cos of diseases', announced Henry importantly. Grandma found an old sock for the puppy to play with and they all watched her pouncing on it and shaking it. 'Have you got any ice-cream?', asked Harry after a bit. 'Ah', replied Grandma, remembering. 'There might be a problem.'

Why did Grandma say there might be a problem? What could the problem be? How can it be sorted out? How do you know? What clues tell you so?

Story 2

Jill's neighbour, Mark, gave her a cherry from the little tree in his front garden. It was dark red, sweet and juicy. 'Delicious', said Jill. 'I might get a cherry tree myself. I could plant it in a big pot I should think.' She dropped the stone into a flower pot as they stood chatting over the fence. That autumn Jill was sorting out the garden, taking out the plants that would not survive the winter. 'What's this?', she said to herself, looking at a small green shoot in a half-filled pot.

What do think Jill has found? How did it get there? How do you know? What clues tell you so?

Reading Between the Lines Set Two

Story 3

Maggie and Ross bought ice-creams and sat on a bench on the cliff path to eat them. Gulls wheeled around overhead and the sun shone. 'Look, out there', said Ross. He pointed at some dark shapes in the sea. 'Do you think they are seals?' Maggie balanced her ice-cream cone between the slats on the bench and reached in her rucksack for the binoculars. She laughed. 'No, silly, have a look for yourself!' Ross took the binoculars and realized that they were surfers. Maggie turned to pick up her ice-cream and found there was only an empty cone.

What is Maggie's problem? What do you think might have happened? How do you know? What clues tell you so?

Story 4

Sean drove the tractor and trailer back to the farm, past the playing fields. His sons, Eddie and Seth, were playing football in the playing field. Seth did a huge kick and the ball disappeared over the wooden fence. He and Eddie looked for ages but couldn't find it. In the end, they went home, fed up. When they walked into the yard, Dad came up to them, grinning. 'Look what I've found!', he said.

What had Dad found? What do you think had happened? How do you know? What clues tell you so?

Story 5

Poppy, the yellow Labrador, had just come back from a great walk. She'd found lots of mud to roll in and now looked filthy. As she got to the back door she saw a bucket, a hosepipe and a bottle of shampoo. She took one look and bounded off as fast as she could. Mason called after her, muttering to himself: 'Well you're not coming in the house until we've done it.'

Why is Poppy running away? Why won't Mason let her in the house? What is Mason planning to do? How do you know? What clues tell you so?

Part 1 - Cause and effect

Story 6

Mason was busy painting the fence. It would definitely look better white. Poppy, the yellow Labrador, was lying in the shade watching him. Just then, Mrs Higgins next door called over the fence. 'Mason, could you give me a hand with this bag of compost, please?' While Mason was next door, Poppy saw Mrs Higgins' ginger cat. She leaped to her feet to chase it. When Mason came back the tin of paint was on its side and a puddle of paint covered the path. Poppy was nowhere to be seen but there were white footprints across the lawn leading to the back door.

Why is the can of paint on its side? Where do you think Poppy is? How is Mason going to find her? What problem could there be in the house? How do you know? What clues tell you so?

Level 4

Story 1

Jennie was making strawberry jam. She stood watching it boil when the doorbell went. It was a parcel for next door but they were out. As Jennie was walking back into the kitchen, she could smell burning.

What happened while Jennie was at the front door? Why is there a smell of burning? How do you know? What clues tell you so?

Story 2

Two-year-old Nathan was playing in the garden while his Mum hung the washing on the line. She looked round and was horrified to see him chewing something. In his hand was an empty snail shell.

Why does Mum look horrified? What has Nathan done? What clues tell you so?

Reading Between the Lines Set Two

Story 3

As she pulled into the supermarket carpark, her phone went. It was her brother-in-law, telling her the baby had been born. She did the shopping in a bit of a daze, feeling very excited. When she got back to the car there was a yellow envelope on the bonnet.

What is in the yellow envelope? What mistake did the woman make? What will she need to do next? Why do you think she made that mistake? How do you know? What clues tell you so?

Story 4

Harrison's arm was in plaster and his knees were covered in plasters. He lay on the sofa watching YouTube clips on his tablet. His skateboard stood propped against the wall.

What had happened to Harrison? What kind of video clips do you think he is watching? How do you know? What clues tell you so?

Story 5

Hansel and Gretel's father took them to the woods to abandon them. But Hansel scattered a trail of breadcrumbs so they could find their way back. As they walked deep into the forest, a flock of little birds followed them.

Why are the birds following them? Can the children now find their way home? How do you know? What clues tell you so?

Story 6

Ross' Granny always fed the birds in her garden, filling the feeders with 'Garden Bird Seed'. 'Granny, why's there a sunflower growing in your grass?', asked six-year-old Ross one day in early summer. 'No idea, Ross, I certainly didn't plant it', replied Granny.

Why is the sunflower growing there? How does Ross know it's a sunflower? How do you know? What clues tell you so?

Part 1 – Cause and effect

Story 7

Muffin was a small tabby cat that couldn't resist an open window. Mrs Winter, who lived next door, locked her back door and went to bed. She was woken in the night by a crashing noise. Feeling nervous, she crept downstairs to find the kitchen bin on its side and rubbish all over the floor.

Why was the bin on the floor? Why was Mrs Winter nervous? How do you know? What clues tell you so?

Story 8

The three friends waited to check in at the airport. At last, it was their turn. 'Um, there's a problem with this passport', said the woman on the desk. Kelly looked in horror at a picture of her partner, Jez Allport.

Why is Kelly looking in horror? What mistake has she made? How do you know? What clues tell you so?

Story 9

'Put three in the bag', said the woman at the garden centre. Later that year, Sahira had her grandchildren over. 'Wow, Nana, there's loads!', exclaimed the children, digging deep into the bag. 'Well, we can roast them for lunch', replied Sahira.

What did Sahira put in the bag? What were there loads of? What do you think they had for lunch? How do you know? What clues tell you so?

Reading Between the Lines Set Two

Story 10

The ever popular Jaz was surrounded by friends as they gathered by the riverside. Further downstream, Mischa sat watching the water, alone as usual. From the distance, she heard a screech. A few seconds later, she reached into the water and retrieved a phone.

Who screamed? Why? Whose phone did Mischa pull from the water? How do you know? What clues tell you so?

Story 11

Number 42 had been empty for ages. 'They'll never sell that', said Liam's Mum. Liam and his mates used to hang out in the overgrown garden. One day, Liam looked out of the window and saw a huge lorry.

Why is there a huge lorry outside? What do you think is in the lorry? How do you know? What clues tell you so?

Story 12

Amy bought a raffle ticket. The first prize was a ticket to an Ed Sheeran concert. She was with her friend Axel when a text pinged on her phone. Amy's face lit up.

Who is Amy's favourite singer? Why did her face light up? How do you know? What clues tell you so?

Time/era

Level 1   132

Level 2   136

Level 3   139

Level 4   142

Level 1

Spot the clues that tell you WHEN SOMETHING HAPPENED OR WILL HAPPEN.

Clues might be about:

- The time of day
- The time of year
- The day or month
- A special day or festival
- A particular period in history

Here is an example. The clues are in bold type.

She pulled on a fleece and padded down to the kitchen. It was **hardly light** as she let the dog out. The **lunch boxes were done** and **backpacks lined up by the door**. On the table were bowls, plates, cutlery and **cereal** boxes. She put some **bread in the toaster** and got the butter and yogurt out of the fridge. Then she put the kettle on and popped a teabag into a mug that said 'Keep Calm and Carry On'. 'Ha Ha', she thought as she called upstairs to the **still sleeping family**.

What time of day is this? How do you know?

- *It's hardly light*
- *She's in the kitchen*
- *Lunch boxes are made and backpacks ready*
- *Toast is being made*
- *The rest of the family are still asleep*

    = *It must be early morning*

Part 1 - Time/era

Story 1

The maths lesson had dragged on and on. This week Class 5 were learning how to calculate the area of different sized rectangles. Emma found it very confusing and she was very relieved when **the bell went**. She and her friends filed out of the class and took their place at the end of the long queue outside the hall. 'What have we got this **afternoon**, Em?', asked her friend Cassie as they waited for the doors to open. 'Science, then art, with that new supply teacher', replied Emma. 'Oh come on, Key Stage 1, hurry up', she muttered impatiently. **Breakfast** seemed a **long time ago** and she was **starving**.

What time of day do you think it is? How do you know? What clues tell you so?

Story 2

'Can you take Bess for a run please, Noah?', called his Nan. Noah looked out at the **grey sky** and sighed. He put on his coat and reached for the dog's lead. Bess stood wagging her tail enthusiastically as Noah clipped the lead to her collar. As he opened the door, an **icy blast of wind** whistled through the hallway. 'And can you call in at the shop and pick up my magazine?', called his Nan from the front room. She turned back to the antiques programme on the TV. 'Bother', thought Noah. He had planned to just nip round the block but a trip to the shop was twice as far. He stepped out into the **cold street** pulling up his collar against the wind. Bess wanted to sniff at every plant and gatepost. 'Come on Bess', said Noah. 'It'll soon be **dark**.'

What time of year do you think it is? What time of day is it? How do you know? What clues tell you so?

Reading Between the Lines Set Two

Story 3

Married women stayed at home much of the time. At home, the women spent much of their time spinning thread and weaving cloth. They looked after the children and prepared food. The women wore a long tunic, called a **chiton**, made from a piece of cotton or linen material that reached their ankles. Rich women went out only with a slave, perhaps to visit women friends. In Athens, only poor women went shopping alone. Their diet was very healthy. They grew wheat and made breads and cereals and noodles. They grew **olives and figs and grapes**. They grew all kinds of vegetables. They kept goats for milk and cheese. Many beautiful **temples** were built to worship their gods. The most important god was **Zeus**.

What period in history do you think this passage is about? How do you know? What clues tell you so?

If you are not sure, how could you find out more information?

Story 4

The two girls woke early. Rosie had come for a sleepover the night before and today Poppy's Mum had promised to take them **swimming in the morning**. Poppy's Mum and Dad were going out in the evening because it was their wedding anniversary. So Poppy was having a sleepover at Rosie's that night. She loved going to Rosie's house because there were two sweet little black kittens to play with. Rosie said they might go for a picnic if the weather was fine **the next day**. The girls dressed and went downstairs to have some breakfast. 'Isn't it lovely to have **two days doing what we want**?', commented Poppy as she spread peanut butter on her toast. Rosie's Mum was talking to Poppy's Mum on the phone. 'Lovely, but I don't want her back **late** because she'll need to wash her hair and it's an **early start** in the morning.'

What part of the week do you think this is about? How do you know? What clues tell you so?

Part 1 - Time/era

Story 5

Tom put on his running gear, did up his trainers and set off. The rest of the household were **still asleep**. It was fine outside but quite cold. Still, after he'd run a couple of kilometres, Tom had definitely warmed up. There were only three weeks to go before the half-marathon so he needed to keep up the training and this was by far the best **time of day**, with **no one around** and very **little traffic**. He decided to do the circular route this time, finishing with the uphill stretch back to the house. As he reached the back door, a delicious **smell of bacon** wafted out and Tom suddenly realized how hungry he was.

What time of day do you think Tom is doing his run? What meal is he coming back to? How do you know? What clues tell you so?

Story 6

Luca said goodbye to his friends and set off for home. He calculated that the journey would take about 30 minutes at this **time of day** when there was **nothing much on the road**. How wrong he was! He'd only gone about three miles when the car started to splutter and then the engine completely cut out. Luca looked at the petrol gauge. Completely out of fuel! And here he was, in the middle of nowhere! There was nothing for it; he'd have to walk the rest of the way. Luckily, he had a **flashlight** on his phone but he couldn't keep it on all the time because the battery was running out. So on he plodded, hoping that perhaps a car would stop and give him a lift. After a while, it started to rain making the whole experience even more unpleasant. By the time he reached his house, which was on the edge of the village, there was a **glimmer of light on the horizon**.

What time of day did Luca set off for home? What was the glimmer of light on the horizon? How do you know? What clues tell you so?

Copyright material from Catherine Delamain & Jill Spring (2018), *Reading Between the Lines Set Two*, Routledge

Reading Between the Lines Set Two

Level 2

Story 1

Most people lived along the banks of the river where they could grow crops and catch fish. Their **houses were made of mud**, with **flat roofs**. People would sleep on the flat roofs in very hot weather. Boys went to school and learnt the symbols, called '**hieroglyphs**', for reading and writing. Girls usually stayed at home and learnt how to cook, spin and keep house. The king or queen was called a **pharaoh**. Most pharaohs were men but some well-known pharaohs were women. A pharaoh was the most important and powerful person in the kingdom. When a pharaoh died, the people placed the body in a **pyramid**.

What period in history do you think this story is about? How do you know? What clues tell you so?

Story 2

Grace **opened her eyes and yawned**. Sun was streaming through the window and the garden was full of **birds singing**. She made a cup of tea and sat in the conservatory. On the other side of the path, a **blackbird was pulling a worm** from the flower bed. The **daffodils** were looking their best and in a little while the **tulips** would be out. Grace loved this time of year, when the **new leaves** were that amazing, fresh green colour and there was **blossom** on the trees in the street. Grace had a little pond at the end of the garden. When she went out to look in it, she was delighted to see that the frogspawn had hatched into **tadpoles**.

What season is it? What time of day is it? How do you know? What clues tell you so?

Part 1 - Time/era

Story 3

Life in England's big cities was dangerous, with **bombs being dropped nearly every day**. Children were **sent to the country** where they would be safe. They travelled by train, carrying their suitcase and **gas mask**. Many of them went to places such as Devon, Cornwall or Wales. When they arrived they were met by a '**billeting officer**', who would choose a **suitable family for each child**. Many of the children had never been outside their home city and, although they missed their families, there were lots of new experiences. They found out where milk and eggs come from and how to grow vegetables. They kept in touch with their families by writing letters home.

What period of English history do you think this is about? How do you know? What clues tell you so?

Story 4

Daisy looked at the clock. Another 15 minutes before the bell would go. Then she'd get a chance to **catch up with Abby and Layla** and find out what was happening about the sleepover. She hoped that Abby's Mum had agreed to both girls staying over on Friday night. They'd planned to do their nails and braid their hair, ready for Abby's birthday trip to the cinema on Saturday. 'So, Daisy, what do *you* think it was like being a girl in Roman times?', said Mr Bradshaw. Of course, Daisy hadn't been listening to a word her history teacher was saying. Ever since they'd **come in from assembly**, she'd been thinking about the sleepover. Luckily, at that very moment, **the bell went** and the class filed **out onto the playground**.

What time of day do you think this is? Why did they file out onto the playground? How do you know? What clues tell you so?

Reading Between the Lines Set Two

Story 5

Billy woke up feeling excited and nervous at the same time. His **uniform** was laid out on the chair in the corner of the room. His **backpack was packed**, including the new **Star Wars pencil case** his Nan had got him. 'Come on Billy', called his Mum from downstairs. 'You don't want to miss the bus on the **first day**!' Billy got dressed, ate his breakfast and set off to the bus stop on the corner of Rosemary Street. It was sunny and a bit cold. He noticed the leaves on the conker tree by the bus stop were a bit brown. Billy was pleased to see his friends had **saved him a place** on the back seat. It was good to see them after so long. 'Wonder what it's going to be like **in Miss Drew's** class', said Ross. 'She's quite strict', replied Billy. 'And **this year the work's much harder**.'

When do you think this is happening? How do you know? What clues tell you so?

Story 6

Nessa's Mum had to go to Leeds on a course so Nessa was staying at Mina's for two nights. She liked staying at Mina's because Mina had a rabbit and a guinea pig. Nessa and her Mum lived in a flat and the landlord didn't allow pets. As soon as they got in **after school**, the girls went into the garden and put Hoppy and Squeak in the run on the grass. Mina's cat sat looking hopeful on the garden bench. Nessa picked some dandelions and fed the little animals through the wire. Just then Mina's Mum appeared. 'Have you girls **got any homework?**', she asked. Mina made a face and sighed. 'History', she replied. 'We've got to spend half an hour reading about Elizabeth the First and making notes.' 'Well, it's **half past five** now', said her Mum. 'If you start now, you'll finished **in time for tea**.'

What time are the girls going to have tea? How do you know? What clues tell you so?

Part 1 - Time/era

Level 3

In the next stories, you have to *find the clues yourself.*

Story 1

They lived in round houses with thatched roofs made of straw or heather. The walls of their houses were made from local material. Houses in the south tended to be made from wattle (woven wood) and daub (straw and mud) as there was an ample supply of wood from the forests. There was a fire in the centre of the round house, which was always kept burning. The smoke escaped through the roof but it still must have been very smoky inside. They didn't have any furniture and slept on animal furs to keep warm. Cooking was done in a huge pot that hung over the fire. The only piece of furniture was a large loom. During the winter, they wove fabric for their clothes on the loom. They used wool from their sheep, which the women would spin, using a spindle. In the evenings, they enjoyed making music, singing and storytelling.

What period in history do you think this is about? Which people are being described? How do you know? What clues tell you so?

Story 2

Tom's Grandad was a farmer. Tom loved going to stay on the farm in the school holidays. They would sit together in the 'maintenance pod' watching the fleet of driverless tractors tilling the land on the big screen. Grandad sometimes let Tom use the electronic control pad to re-programme the vehicles or direct them to a different part of the land. It was cosy in the pod and everything was available via the series of touch screens. If you wanted a hot drink, you just hovered your finger over the type of drink on the green screen. Then a few seconds later, the drink would appear in a special canister, at just the right temperature. Tom loved it best when Grandad told me about the old days, when he used to sit in something called the 'cab' and drive the tractor by steering a big wheel and pushing pedals with his feet.

When do you think this story is set? How do you know? What clues tell you so?

Reading Between the Lines Set Two

Story 3

As soon as they'd finished tea, Evie and Fran put on warm coats, scarves, gloves and boots. Dad got the big torch out of the cupboard under the stairs and they set off, up the hill to the playing field. It had been raining earlier but, luckily, now it seemed to have stopped. There was already quite a crowd when they arrived. Dad paid the entrance fee and they strolled over to a van selling hot dogs and toffee apples. 'Hurry up and make up your minds girls, it's going to start in a minute!', said Dad. Carrying their toffee apples, they joined the main crowd in the centre of the playing field. There was a crackling noise as Alf Trendle and Ron Legg lit the dry sticks. Soon after there was a 'Whoosh!' and everyone looked up at the spray of coloured sparks high in the sky.

What time of year is this? What date do you think it might be? How do you know? What clues tell you so?

Story 4

The special assembly seemed to go on forever. Harrison gazed out of the window towards the playing fields as Mr Lofting read out an endless list of pupils who'd got prizes or certificates of some sort. Harrison stood up when his names was called and everyone clapped because he'd won the long jump on sports day. Harrison couldn't believe that sports day was already two weeks ago. Each day since then seemed to go more slowly than the last. The long hot afternoons were the worst Harrison decided, remembering the droning voice of Mr Jones, going into great detail about daily life as a Victorian child. But, never mind, only another 20 minutes to go, thought Harrison, dragging himself back into the present. Then six weeks of freedom – he could hardly wait!

What time of year do you think it is? Why does Harrison think 'six weeks of freedom'? Which day in the school term do you think it is? How do you know? What clues tell you so?

Part 1 - Time/era

Story 5

Beth Crossley was dreaming she was walking through a forest following a white pony. She came to a clearing and the pony stopped to graze. For some reason, there was a table with a cup and saucer on it. Next to the cup was a tin. As Beth approached the table, the tin began to shake and make an ear-splitting sound. The sound got louder and louder and suddenly Beth woke up and sat bolt upright in bed. On the little table beside the bed, her alarm clock was buzzing. 'It can't be 6.30 already', thought Beth. 'It's not even light outside.' She silenced the alarm and lay down for a few minutes, thinking about the day ahead. Eventually, she dragged herself out of bed and pulled the curtains. There was a glimmer of light creeping over the rooftops. 'Oh well', she thought. 'At least I had a lovely weekend!'

What day of the week do you think it is? What time of day is it? How do you know? What clues tell you so?

Story 6

Irina heaved a sigh of relief as she bolted the door and put up the 'CLOSED' sign. She sorted out the day's takings and put the cash in the plastic envelope ready to take to the bank. Then she locked the back door and washed up the mugs that had gathered in the sink. After checking everything was in its place, she locked the door and walked down to the bank. It was a damp chilly evening and the last think Irina wanted to do was go to the supermarket. But she'd promised her partner, Rex, that she'd make his favourite vegetable curry tonight and she knew there was only an onion and a few green beans in the fridge. 'Anyway', she thought, 'if I do it now I won't have to do it on Saturday.'

What day of the week is it? What time of day is it? How do you know? What clues tell you so?

Reading Between the Lines Set Two

Level 4

Story 1

This was an era when many new things were invented, including the bicycle, the camera, postage stamps and the telephone. The queen's bathing machine allowed her to swim in the sea.

What period in history do you think this is about? How do you know? What clues tell you so?

Story 2

It was a beautiful day for a walk in the woods. The sun soon burnt through the early mist, lighting up the yellows, oranges and reds in the trees above.

What season of the year is this about? How do you know? What clues tell you so?

Story 3

It had been a long, hot day and even though it was nearly 10 it was still light enough to read outside.

What season is this about? How do you know? What clues tell you so?

Story 4

The recipe said 'Bake for 30 minutes at 180 degrees.' Elsie looked at her watch. It was quarter past 11.

What time will the dish be finished? How do you know? What clues tell you so?

Part 1 - Time/era

Story 5

It was a great party. On the dot of midnight, they joined hands and sang 'Auld Lang Syne' and the bells in the nearest church chimed.

What time of year is this? What are they celebrating? How do you know? What clues tell you so?

Story 6

He woke at 7.30. It was pitch dark outside and the ground was frosty. He knew he'd have to scrape the windscreen before he left.

What time of day is this? What season of the year? How do you know? What clues tell you so?

Story 7

Pagans, druids and other revellers gathered at Stonehenge in Wiltshire this morning to watch the sunrise in the ancient festival that celebrates fertility, renewal and harvest.

What month is this? What season of the year is it? What is the festival called? How do you know? What clues tell you so?

Story 8

The queen reigned for 44 years, which in those days was a long time. The defeat of the Spanish ushered England into an age of prosperity, peace, and expansion.

What period in history is this sentence about? How do you know? What clues tell you so?

Reading Between the Lines Set Two

Story 9

On Monday afternoon, Joan, the owner of the shop, asked Becky if she could do an extra shift the day after tomorrow.

Which day is Becky doing the extra shift? How do you know? What clues tell you so?

Story 10

They also built grand country houses called 'villas'. These had many rooms, some with beautifully painted walls, mosaic floors and even central heating.

What period in history is the writer describing? How do you know? What clues tell you so?

Story 11

On Saturday, she went into the music shop on the High Street and bought a vinyl single of 'Please Please Me!' by the Beatles.

What decade is the writer talking about? How do you know? What clues tell you so?

Story 12

Lola and Jess waited impatiently for the 10.30 train. They were meeting their friend Ellie in town and Ellie's Mum was going to take them to the cinema. 'What time will we get there?', asked Jess. 'Well, it takes 40 minutes on the train', replied Lola.

What time will they arrive? How do you know? What clues tell you so?

Part 2

Lucky dip

Lucky dip

Story 1

It was busy today. 'School holidays', she thought as a mother and daughter staggered in with an enormous bin liner. 'That's so kind', she said, lugging the bag to the back. She'd sold several puzzles, a vase and a book about steam trains.

Where is this taking place? Why did she say 'school holidays'? How do you know? What clues tell you so?

Story 2

Maddie was on her mobile. 'Well, tell her we're doing homework at mine or something', she muttered, looking over her shoulder to make sure her Mum wasn't listening.

Who do you think Maddie is talking to? Is she telling the truth? Why doesn't she want her mum to hear? How do you know? What clues tell you so?

Story 3

She looked in the window every afternoon on the way home from school. The small black one edged towards her pressing its nose against the glass. 'If only', she thought.

What do you think she is looking at? Why does she say 'If only'? What is pressing its nose against the glass? How do you know? What clues tell you so?

Reading Between the Lines Set Two

Story 4

'Red Group this end, Blue Group the far end', barked the instructor. Ravi picked up his goggles and walked reluctantly to the edge.

Where do you think Ravi is? Why does he need goggles? Does he enjoy this activity? How do you know? What clues tell you so?

Story 5

It was so hot standing there, chopping. Chen felt like he'd been chopping for ever but the pile never seemed to get smaller. 'Four Number 24s with extra rice and onion', he heard his Auntie call from the front.

Where is Chen? What could he be chopping? What is his Auntie doing? How do you know? What clues tell you so?

Story 6

Beth walked into the house, expecting to be greeted by a warm, savoury smell. But the kitchen was chilly. She walked over to the cooker. Stone cold. 'But I'm sure I set the timer this morning', she thought.

Why was Beth expecting a warm savoury smell? Why was the cooker stone cold? What had Beth forgotten to do? How do you know? What clues tell you so?

Story 7

'Have you got anything today – I've been awake since 2 am and it's so swollen I can hardly speak.' 'He'll fit you in as an emergency this afternoon, but you'll probably have to wait', replied the receptionist

Who does this person want to see? Why has she been awake since 2 am? Why can she hardly speak? How do you know? What clues tell you so?

Part 2 – Lucky dip

Story 8

She let Suki out and went over to the basket. There were four of them, nestling like little moles, eyes tight shut, little feet scrabbling about. 'You clever girl Suki', she said, pouring some milk into a saucer.

What is Suki? What are the creatures in the basket? Why are their eyes tight shut? How do you know? What clues tell you so?

Story 9

'At last', thought Ahmed. He got on and headed for the back seat where his friends had kept him a space. 'You done your homework, Medi?', asked his friend Raki.

What did Ahmed 'get on'? Where is he going? How do you know? What clues tell you so?

Story 10

On the list, it said 'ground coriander' but he couldn't see any. When he asked the girl on the checkout, she just shrugged and said 'Dunno'. He sighed. If he didn't get it, she wouldn't be able to make it.

Where is he? What do you think she might be going to make? How do you know? What clues tell you so?

Story 11

'Opening times 10.00–16.30.' Cara looked at the huge turreted house. 'Right', she thought, 'I've got about an hour.'

Where do you think Cara is? What time is it? What does she have to do in one hour? How do you know? What clues tell you so?

Copyright material from Catherine Delamain & Jill Spring (2018), *Reading Between the Lines Set Two*, Routledge

Reading Between the Lines Set Two

Story 12

Grandpa Joe looked very pale as he climbed the little ladder into the basket. He wished he'd never said this was on his bucket list. But 10 minutes later, he stood amazed as he saw his house, like a toy, way down below.

How old do you think Grandpa Joe is? What is he climbing into? Why did he wish it wasn't on his bucket list? Why does his house look like a toy? How do you know? What clues tell you so?

Story 13

'Well stop at a shop on the way home, then', she snapped. 'You know how much Nana puts on her cereal.'

What has the person got to get at the shop? What does Nana need on her cereal? Do you think Nana lives with these people? How do you know? What clues tell you so?

Story 14

Carlo was late again. By the time he got there, they were all lined up along the side, ready to do their first length. He changed as quickly as he could but then realized he hadn't got his goggles.

Where is Carlo? Where are the others lined up? How will he manage without his goggles? How do you know? What clues tell you so?

Story 15

She'd been looking forward to it for ages and at last the day had arrived. Sitting in the back of the taxi, she thought about the pool, the entertainment, the shops and the beach.

What has she been looking forward to? Why is she in a taxi? Where is it taking her? How do you know? What clues tell you so?

Part 2 – Lucky dip

Story 16

Wei Lin had always hated the smell in these places. He asked the young woman in a pale blue uniform where to go. He couldn't believe the shrivelled little creature in the bed was Ma, who only a week ago was arguing with the neighbours and cooking her own food.

What kind of place does Wei Lin hate the smell of? Who is he visiting? What do you think has happened to Ma? How do you know? What clues tell you so?

Story 17

They queued for popcorn, which Mum said was overpriced. 'But it is my treat', pleaded Chrissie as they took their seats just before the lights went down. When they came out it was dark and raining.

Why is it Chrissie's treat? Where are they? What time of day do they go into this place? What time of year do you think it is? Why is it dark when they come out? How do you know? What clues tell you so?

Story 18

'But I HAVE to watch it, RIGHT NOW!', screeched four-year-old Nathan, throwing himself on the floor. Finn rootled about in the drawer in the kitchen and sighed. 'Sorry, Nath, it needs three A3s.'

Why is Nathan cross? What is Finn looking for? What is it that they haven't got? How do you know? What clues tell you so?

Story 19

Rufus saw something shiny above him on the table. First, he shuffled, then, he managed to stand up and totter towards it. But, as he reached up to grab it, his little legs gave way and he sat down hard.

How old do you think Rufus is? What do you think is on the table? Why does he suddenly sit down? How do you know? What clues tell you so?

Reading Between the Lines Set Two

Story 20

The hut on the playing field had always been derelict, she thought. Empty, full of spiders and cobwebs and rotting garden furniture. So why was there a pair of shoes, a flask and a sleeping bag on the path outside?

Do you think someone has inhabited the shed? Where has the person gone? Why did they leave their stuff? How do you know? What clues tell you so?

Story 21

Ivan could just see the wretched thing glinting under the grating, where it had slipped out of his pocket. Now how was he going to get in? Mum had a spare and so did Dad, but they wouldn't be home till six.

What can Ivan see under the grating? How do you know? What will be his problem if he can't get the thing out? What clues tell you so?

Story 22

Mrs Winter made her way up the broad stairway to Level 2 and turned left for the Children's Ward. Tom was right at the end by the window, his plastered leg stuck out in front of him. He was chuffed to get the latest book about his favourite hero and the packet of chocolate biscuits

Where are Mrs Winter and Tom? How do you know? Is Tom a grown-up or a boy? Why do you think he is in hospital? Did Mrs Winter bring him anything? How do you know? What clues tell you so?

Part 2 - Lucky dip

Story 23

Tessa had put her alarm clock under her pillow, so as not to disturb everybody when she woke. She dressed quietly and crept downstairs as the first light was just beginning to glimmer in the sky. When she reached the hall and smelt frying bacon, she realized that she'd been beaten to it.

When did Tessa get up? How do you know? Was she first up in the house? Who do think was? What clues tell you so?

Story 24

The policeman nodded and nudged the driver. They switched on the blue light and the siren and began to accelerate past the slow-moving cars. The Porsche was still just in sight ahead, weaving recklessly in and out of the traffic and causing furious hooting.

Why did the policemen switch on their light and siren? How do you know? What clues tell you so?

What were they going to do? What sort of car were they chasing? What was it doing wrong?

Story 25

Angus stopped and put his backpack down. 'Whew', he thought. 'That's a good two miles I've done on foot.' He turned to face the traffic, looking for a likely vehicle. Soon a Range Rover pulled in. 'Hop aboard', said the driver, 'if Exeter is any good to you.' Angus cheered.

How is Angus making his journey? How do you know? Has he got much luggage? Where is he going, do you think? What clues tell you so?

Reading Between the Lines Set Two

Story 26

'I'd like to put my name down for three of the races', Bertie said to Mr Andrews. 'Well, there's nothing like ambition', the coach said with a raised eyebrow. Bertie's smile faded. 'Perhaps I'll settle for just one or two', he said.

Why did Bertie change his mind about how many races to enter for? How do you think he felt? How do you know? What clues tell you so?

Story 27

Mandy's face fell as she unwrapped her birthday present from Leah. 'She's used old creased Christmas paper and I saw that book in the shop marked down to half price', she said. 'I thought we were best friends.'

Why was Mandy disappointed with her present? How do you know? What clues tell you so?

What does she mean by saying she thought she and Leah were best friends?

Story 28

Kitty and Johnny said thank you to Ella's Dad as they got out of the car, and started towards the front door. Their Mum had barely opened it when Ella came panting up the path behind them, waving a pair of trainers. 'He's left these behind', she said breathlessly 'and it's nets practice this evening'.

Who had left the trainers behind? How do you know? What clues tell you so?

Will the trainers be needed again later in the day? Why do you think so?

Part 2 - Lucky dip

Story 29

'Well, that wasn't too bad', said Lana, as they handed their papers into the supervisor and made their way out into the corridor. Luisa looked at her in amazement. 'I thought it was worse than the last one', she said. 'There were two questions I didn't even try to answer.'

What have the girls been doing? How do you know? What clues tell you so?

Who do you think will have done better? Have they done an exam before this one?

Story 30

Bertie scowled as he looked out of the window. Only an hour until his match was due to start and it looked as if it would be a mud bath. Last time, it had been this bad and you couldn't tell your own team members from the opposition players.

What did Bertie see when he looked out of the window? How do you know? What clues tell you so?

What is he going to be doing later on? Why might you not be able to tell one team from the other?

Story 31

Ted had his ears to the door where their parents were planning the holiday. 'Dad said this year it would be fun to go when the new lambs are being born', Ted reported, 'and before the tourist invasion starts. Looks like we won't have too long to wait, it's nearly Easter already.'

Who do you think Ted was talking to? When are they going on holiday this year? How do you know? What clues tell you so?

Where are they going to stay? Have they been on a holiday like this before? What did Dad dislike about last year's holiday?

Reading Between the Lines Set Two

Story 32

Allie carefully put the empty eggshell upside down in her brother's eggcup. Ben arrived in a rush as usual, plonked himself down and attacked his egg with a teaspoon. Allie burst out laughing as she saw his expression. 'Fooled you', she cried. 'Look what day it is!'

When might Allie have played this trick on Ben? How do you know? What clues tell you so?

What did Ben discover when he tried to eat his boiled egg?

Story 33

Anna looked through the window at the waves, which seemed to be getting bigger all the time. The movement was getting quite violent. 'Let's go up on deck', said Dad, looking at her white face, 'Fresh air helped last time.'

Where are Anna and her Dad? How do you know? What clues tell you so?

Why did Dad suggest they go up on deck? Has Anna been on a trip like this before?

Story 34

'Two invitations for the same day', said Belle, as she ripped open the envelopes. 'I wouldn't go to Fiona's if it was the grandest bash ever. Might go to Sue's, though. Just as long as it isn't fancy dress.'

Which of the two people who sent her invitations does Belle like best? How do you know? What clues tell you so?

Does she enjoy fancy dress parties?

Part 2 – Lucky dip

Story 35

Susanna's eyes ached from peering through the narrow slit in the hide. Since two o'clock they had seen countless varieties of duck, including teal and widgeon, but never a glimpse of a merganser. In half an hour, by six anyway, it would start getting dark and then it would be too late.

What is Susanna doing? How do you know? What clues tell you so?

Is Susanna on her own? What are they hoping to see? How long have they been there?

Story 36

That evening, the maths homework was horrible. Jared thought he would try the tummy ache trick, but Dad didn't fall for it until Jared said he didn't want any tea. Dad looked at him in astonishment. It worked until Mum came into the kitchen and found Jared sneaking biscuits out of the biscuit tin.

How did Jared try to get out of doing his homework? How do you know? What clues tell you so?

Why did it give the game away when he was found eating biscuits? Do you think he usually had a good appetite? What makes you think so?

Story 37

Dad read the sign by the entrance to the big dipper. 'Rosie, I am so sorry', he said. 'What bad luck. You'll have to do a bit more growing, I'm afraid. We'll go and find something else just as much fun.'

What is Dad sorry about? How do you know? What clues tell you so?

Why can't Rosie go on the big dipper? When will she be able to go on a ride like this?

Copyright material from Catherine Delamain & Jill Spring (2018),
Reading Between the Lines Set Two, Routledge

Reading Between the Lines Set Two

Story 38

The angry mob was surging down the street and getting closer, still yelling and throwing stones at windows. The reporter hastily packed away his camera and phone, but he was satisfied the ringleader would be recognizable from his shot.

Why do you think the reporter hurried to hide his camera and phone? What has he been doing? What did he think might happen? Why was it important that he had got a good shot of the ringleader? How do you know? What clues tell you so?

Story 39

Annabel crossed her fingers as she pressed the 'Send' button. She looked again at the advertisement and wondered for the 100th time whether she had said enough to convince them she was right for it. She always tended to sell herself short.

What sort of message was Annabel sending? How do you know? What clues tell you so?

Was she happy about her message? Has she applied for jobs before, do you think?

Story 40

The man stood and looked at the hill, and measured it with his eyes. In his mind, he compared it with the one he'd climbed yesterday. About the same and not so many tricky bits. After a glance at his watch and a look at the sky, he made up his mind. He'd still be back at the hotel by supper time.

What was the man trying to make up his mind about? Why did he look at his watch? Why did he look at the sky? What did he decide to do? What must have helped him decide? How do you know? What clues tell you so?

Stories

Everyday theme 160

Magical theme 166

Adventure theme 171

Reading Between the Lines Set Two

Everyday theme

Story 1

'At last', thought Amber, slamming it shut. 'Come on, Toby', she called. 'What are you doing now, you promised you'd help.' Eventually a sleepy-looking Toby emerged, pulling on a fleece and eating a piece of toast at the same time. 'Is it all day?', he mumbled. 'Why have we got to go so early?', grumbled Toby, shedding crumbs everywhere. 'We need to get a good place, where we can be seen, as near the entrance as possible', explained Amber. This time, they were lucky. There was a gap between a white van and a Land Rover. Toby put the table up and together they set everything out. They had just about finished when people started to arrive. The next couple of hours were busy and Toby began to enjoy himself. 'You drive a hard bargain, son', commented a middle-aged man in a flat cap. By 11 o'clock there were only a handful of things left. Amber was busy counting, looking pleased with herself. 'Brilliant!', she announced. 'Dinner at Antonio's tonight for you and me!'

What did Amber slam shut? Why do they need to be near the entrance? Why did the man say that Toby 'drives a hard bargain'? What is Toby enjoying? What was Amber counting? Why are they going to Antonio's? How do you know? What clues tell you so?

Part 2 – Stories

Story 2

The appointment was at 10.30. It was now 10.45, so obviously things were running late today. 'I just know what they are going to say', whispered Anna. 'Come on, it might not be that bad', Joe replied, also looking at the wicker basket. After what seemed an age, the door opened and a kind-looking man in a white overall said: 'Anna, Joe and Monty please.' They followed him into a small room. Joe put the wicker basket on the table and looked at the man. 'Hi, I'm Mike, how can I help you today?' Joe indicated the basket and carefully undid the catch. Mike peered inside. Then he said 'I think we need to take a proper look.' He put on some rubber gloves and reached into the basket. 'Come on there, old guy, easy. I'm not going to hurt you.' The examination took about 10 minutes, with Anna and Joe standing side by side, close to each other. Finally, Mike looked them in the eye and said: 'I'm afraid there's not much more we can do, this is the kindest way. I am so so sorry.'

What is in the basket? What did Anna think they were going to say? Why does Mike say he's 'so so sorry'? How do you know? What clues tell you so?

Story 3

Mel loved Boxing Day. Christmas had happened, the pressure was off and now she had time to enjoy the family. Her parents were coming for what they always called 'Boxing Day Lunch'. This meant cold meat, salad and whatever was left over. This year, she'd cooked a big piece of ham, which was now in the utility room covered in foil. It was a lovely morning so they decided to go for a walk with Alfie first thing. Tilly and Finn were excited about seeing Gramps and Nana, knowing there were still some things under the tree. They didn't really want to go for a walk but, as Tilly said, 'it makes the time go by!' When they got back Alfie went straight to the garden shed. At that moment, a green Nissan Micra pulled up beside the house and the children rushed out to greet them. Inside the house, Mel looked in horror into the utility room. Where was it? On the top of the washing machine were telltale paw prints. Mel ran to the shed where she found Alfie and Dots fast asleep.

Who is Alfie? Why were the children excited about seeing their grandparents? What was Mel looking for in the utility room? What is the family cat called? What do you think happened to the ham? How do you know? What clues tell you so?

Copyright material from Catherine Delamain & Jill Spring (2018), *Reading Between the Lines Set Two*, Routledge

Reading Between the Lines Set Two

Story 4

Nadya put it in the oven and set the timer for 35 minutes. Then she got to work on the next one. This one was in a tray and seemed less likely to collapse. While she was waiting for the first one, she got out some plastic storage containers ready to put them in. Then she found a wire cooling rack and at that moment the timer beeped. Nervously, she opened the oven door – not bad, she thought, carefully taking it out and putting the tray one in. At that moment, her phone rang. It was Bethany Holder, who insisted on telling Nadya that she'd done four already and had three more in the oven and please could Nadya take Aleesha to Brownies tonight. 'No problem', said Nadya, secretly wishing she'd never agreed to this fund raiser. Still, it would be amazing to have a year-round pool at the school.

What is Nadya making? What is Bethany making? Why is she nervous? What is the school raising funds for? How do you know? What clues tell you so?

Story 5

Rose went out to the greenhouse and opened a large plastic tub. She filled an old plastic jug and walked over to the patio. For the third morning in a row, the peanut feeder was on the ground. Rose sighed as she hung it back on its hook. 'Must be those starlings squabbling over the nuts', she thought to herself. She filled the other two feeders up and went back into the house. Within a couple of minutes, a cluster of sparrows appeared, followed by a very large pigeon and, as usual, the bossy starlings. Just then, the phone rang. It was Rose's neighbour, Mark. 'Go up to your bathroom and look out of the window', he said. Rose did as she was told, taking the phone with her. From the bathroom, she could see both her garden and Mark's. 'Look', Mark said, 'Right there by my garage door. I saw it come over your fence just a minute ago.' 'Ughhh! That's horrible', replied Rose. 'I'm going to ring the council right now!' She hung up and looked up the number to call. 'That explains why the peanut feeder was on the ground', she thought to herself.

What did Rose keep in the plastic tub? What did Mark see climbing over Rose's fence? Why did Rose ring the council? What do you think will happen next? Why was the peanut feeder on the ground? How do you know? What clues tell you so?

Story 6

It started to rain, a steady penetrating drizzle. As the drops fell on the fire, it fizzled and began to go out, so they all went to bed early. They were looking forward to trying out the grand new super-traveller, which had separate compartments, built-in groundsheets and double thickness canvas. It was much better than the old one and Dad hoped it would even convert Mum to this kind of holiday. Anya was just drifting off to sleep when a drip fell on her nose and she could see rain seeping through the canvas above her. She grabbed her torch and went to find a bucket. She had just groped her way back to her sleeping bag when something huge and heavy stumbled over one of the guy ropes and uttered a startled 'moo'. 'Not much sleep for us tonight', Anya thought, as she went to wake her parents. 'Where there's one there are sure to be more'.

What is the family doing? Have they done this sort of thing before? What did they think was going to be better about this year? What do you think has fallen over the guy rope, and what does Anya think might happen next? Does Mum enjoy camping? Do you think this holiday will make her change her mind? Will Dad be pleased with the new tent, do you suppose? How do you know? What clues tell you so?

Story 7

Damian wasn't sure he wouldn't rather just have gone home as usual at teatime and played on his iPad or chatted to his mates on his phone. But the PE teacher had been so persuasive that he'd agreed to try it for a week and here he was. Inside the hall, there seemed to be a lot going on. Two people were playing table tennis, some others were practising getting the ball into a netball net, there was a pool table and a darts board. The place was crowded and full of cheerful noise. Through the doors at the far end, there even seemed to be a small field with a cricket net. Then he spotted Josh, a friend from his year. 'I didn't know Josh had joined', thought Damian. 'He never mentioned it. I made the right decision'.

Where had Damian gone? Why did he decide to try it?

Had he been expecting to enjoy himself? Did seeing Josh make a difference? Do you think he will go to this place again? How do you know? What clues tell you so?

Reading Between the Lines Set Two

Story 8

'We'll go up to the front on the outside', Mr Rossi said, as they crossed the gangplank. 'We're all well wrapped up and we'll be plenty warm enough'. The tour guide welcomed everybody aboard and Tonio watched the crew casting off the mooring ropes and coiling them down neatly on the deck. The engine gave a hoot as they headed out into the current. 'The first thing we pass will be St Paul's Cathedral on your left', came the guide's voice, 'and after that I'm sure you'll all recognise the Tower. You'll see the water gate where prisoners used to be landed. Some of them were never freed, but died in captivity'. 'Make sure you both get some good photos to show your Grandfather when we get home', said Mrs Rossi, 'You know he's never been to England.' Tonio fished out his phone and Emilia her iPad. There would be the usual argument about who had the better pictures when they got back to the hotel.

What is the Rossi family doing? Can you guess what city they are in? Do you think they live in that city? What time of year do you think it is?

Does Tonio have a brother or sister? How do you know? What clues tell you so?

Story 9

As Oscar walked past the turning into Battery Road, he could see something happening at the far end, where the road petered out into wasteland and abandoned buildings. He and his friends had often played there. Oscar went to join a small crowd, being held back by a rope and a watchful policeman. 'High time', said someone. 'This place is long overdue for development.' A huge bulldozer stood by the old factory and as they watched the arm swung round and the top two stories began to crumble. A noisy avalanche of debris – concrete, metal and glass – cascaded to the ground amid a shower of dust. 'Sad to see it go', said a man standing by Oscar. 'That wasn't just an old building to me – that was my life for 20 years.'

What is the crowd watching? Why is the crowd roped off? Has the building been derelict for long? Is everyone in the crowd glad to see it being knocked down? What does the man mean by saying the building had been his life? How do you know? What clues tell you so?

Part 2 - Stories

Story 10

The coach pulled up by an enormous building. 'Here we are', said Miss Mills, unnecessarily. 'Everybody out. I want you to stay with me for the first half hour and after that you can visit what you like, but stay in pairs or threes. We meet in the entrance hall at 4 o'clock.' Marisha was fascinated by the dinosaurs, particularly the vast diplodocus and she loved the insects and the birds. Miss Mills was brilliant at describing the behaviour of the various creatures and how the food chains worked. When the half hour was up, Marisha and Selina paired off and started out to explore full of enthusiasm. However, by three they were both looking at their watches. 'I can't get my head round these old bones and stuff', Marisha said, and Selina agreed. 'Let's go and grab a coke or a latte in the café.'

What sort of place are these people visiting? Are these grown-ups or children? Who do you think Miss Mills is? How do you think Marisha and Selina were feeling by 3 o'clock? What did the writer mean by saying 'unnecessarily' about Miss Mills' remark? How do you know? What clues tell you so?

Magical theme

Story 1

The young man was holding something out to the girl. It looked like a little cloth bag. She took it and carefully slid her fingers inside. Her eyes shone as she pulled out the contents. The two smiled at each other, a split second of happiness, before the girl's face clouded over and she shook her head. The young man took hold of one of her fingers but she pulled her hand away, talking fast in her strange language. Slowly, he nodded in understanding and stood looking puzzled. Suddenly, he grasped her by the arm and led her to the side of the clearing. He bent down and taking a knife from his belt began hacking at the grass and digging into the earth. He dug fast in the soft peaty soil, until his arm disappeared well above the elbow. The two crouched by the hole and the girl held out the bag. Henri put it to his lips, then slipped it into the hole. Together, they filled the hole and the girl planted an acorn, to mark the spot.

Why did the girl's eyes shine as she took out the contents of the bag? What was in the bag? Why did she pull her hand away? Why don't the two people speak the same language? When do you think this story is happening? Why did they dig the hole? Why did they plant an acorn? What will the acorn turn into? How do you know? What clues tell you so?

Story 2

I stood quite still. I felt as if I was paralysed, caught between the past and the present with no control over either, just watching while history trudged its cruel uncaring way. I looked without seeing at the path the girl had taken, her last journey. And as I gazed dreamily ahead a sudden sound made me look, instantly alert. It sounded like a cross between a hiss and a whistle. I looked up but saw nothing and then, all of a sudden, the sound stopped, extinguished in a soft thud, followed by a dragging, rustling noise, then silence. I put my hand to my mouth. My teeth were chattering, my fingers shaking and I thought I might be sick. There was no mistaking what I had heard. It was the final moment of the legend of the Three Gold Rings.

Why does the writer say she is 'caught between the present and the past?' What happened to the girl? Why was it her last journey? What do you think the whistling noise was? Why did it stop? How do you know? What clues tell you so?

Part 2 - Stories

Story 3

'Look at that, Burt', said Ivy Potter, handing him the copy of the local paper as she got ready to go to work. He put down his toast, picked up his reading glasses and read '£500 REWARD FOR THE RETURN OF MY GRANDFATHER'S WATCH'. The contact address was Chatto House, where Ivy worked as a cleaner. Today, when she arrived Mrs Holmes, the housekeeper, gave her a list of duties. They included polishing the panelling in the room they called the Snug. Ivy collected the cleaning kit and made her way down to the Snug. She'd get that job done first as it always took longest. The Snug was a small, quiet room, with several paintings of Chatto ancestors on the walls. She started on the East Wall, carefully rubbing in the beeswax polish before polishing it with the special duster. She'd just reached the panel by the doorway when there was a clicking sound. Ivy lifted the duster and to her amazement saw the panel silently glide back, revealing a space. She peered into the dark space but it seemed empty. Or did it? Right at the back, almost out of sight, something caught the light.

Who has lost something? What was the name of that person's grandfather? What made the panel slide open? What do you think might be in the back of the space? How do you know? What clues tell you so?

Story 4

Lisa lived with her Mum and Dad in a small village. Lisa's Nan lived at the other end of the street, past the playground. Lisa liked going round to Nan's because she had lots of interesting ornaments and she always had some sweets for Lisa. Nan couldn't walk very well since she fell over on the ice, so Lisa's Mum did her shopping for her. One morning, Mum asked Lisa to take it round to Nan's. It was a really cold morning, so Lisa put on her red fleece and set off. When she got to the playground she saw some of her friends hanging out by the swings and she wanted to go and join them. She put the Tesco bag down, but a very large, grey dog came up and sniffed at it. So she decided she'd better take the shopping to Nan's first. The dog lolloped along beside her. It really was huge, with grey spiky fur, no collar and pointed teeth. Lisa felt a bit nervous and decided not to pat it or anything. At the edge of the park, Lisa stopped to text her friend, Ella. She didn't notice the dog bounding off, in the direction of Nan's house. When Lisa arrived at Nan's house she was surprised to see the door open. Nan was very fussy about locking doors.

Why did Lisa feel nervous? Why didn't she touch the dog? Why do you think Nan's door was open? Does this story remind you of anything you might have read before? How do you know? What clues tell you so?

Reading Between the Lines Set Two

Story 5

His house was on the hill, outside the village, just by the bus stop. The village children used to make faces and throw stones into his garden while they waited for the school bus. This annoyed him a lot. In his kitchen, there was a big old pot, stained black after years of use. He'd get down an old book with a leather cover and peer at the thin pages, making notes on the back of a cereal packet. 'Smack!' Another stone hit his front door, followed by laughter. 'That's it', he said to himself. He reached up to the shelf by the cooker and took down some little jars. Then he went over to the table where the battered old book lay open, on page 104. 'Ah', he said, stepping outside the back door and scooping something into a little tin and closing the lid. There was a small tapping sound from inside the tin. He spooned powder from the jars into the pan, then poured in water. Once it was boiling, he emptied the contents of the little tin into the pot. If you had walked up the hill the next morning, you might have noticed a little procession of scruffy-looking rats making their way past the house. But there were no children waiting at the bus stop.

What do you think he was making in the old pot? What kind of book do you think it was? What did he put in the tin? Why were there rats walking past his house? Why were there no children waiting for the school bus? How do you know? What clues tell you so?

Story 6

Jo and Daisy trailed round behind their parents in the huge house. They had started in the Great Hall and had now reached the Long Gallery. They were half-listening to their audio guides, but were mostly just longing for lunch. The tour stopped by the portrait of a beautiful queen. Daisy's audio guide said quietly in her ear: 'This queen was executed.' The lady in the picture took off her head and tucked it under her arm. Amazed, Daisy looked at Jo. Had he seen it too? Yes, Jo was staring at the picture with his mouth open. The rest of the group didn't seem to have noticed a thing. 'This king had to hide from his enemies in a tree', came the voice in her ear again, as they moved on to the next picture. King Charles got down from his throne and began to scramble into the branches of a huge oak.

What are Jo and Daisy and their parents doing? What is the magic that happened? Where was the magic coming from? Have the rest of the group got audio guides, do you think? Will Jo and Daisy be likely to remember anything about these kings and queens? How do you think they will feel about visits to stately homes and castles in the future? How do you know? What clues tell you so?

Part 2 - Stories

Story 7

The supply teacher was an odd-looking man, with wild grey hair and lopsided wire-framed glasses. 'I understand this class is trouble', he said. 'I am going to sort you out once and for all.' The children waited in happy anticipation. He wasn't the first to try to tame Class 8. Mr Strange brought his hand out of his pocket, there was a flash and on every chair in the room sat a mouse instead of a child. Next Mr Strange produced a large ferocious-looking cat, which began to prowl menacingly among the trembling mice. Mr Strange went to the door. 'I'm going for my coffee break now', he announced. 'I will be back in 15 minutes.' Silence reigned in the classroom, apart from the soft padding of the cat's feet and a nervous gasp from one of the mice when the cat stopped beside it.

Had Class 8 been badly behaved for a long time? Had other teachers tried to control them? Were the children looking forward to outwitting this teacher as well? What magic did Mr. Strange make happen? Were the mice frightened of the cat? How do you know? What do you think Mr. Strange will say to them when he comes back from his coffee break? Do you think it will make the children better-behaved in the future? How do you know? What clues tell you so?

Story 8

Alicia's Fairy Godmother always gave her a magic Courage Potion on her birthday. She could choose what to turn into and the magic would last exactly the number of hours of her age. This year she had decided to tackle her feelings about swimming. 'Ten hours as a trout should do it if anything will', she said to herself as she stood on the river bank. As she looked at the water, she could see shoals of small fish darting near the bottom. 'Coming to join you', she said as she swallowed the potion down and waited. The magic began to work and she found herself longing to dive in to the cool, clear water. 'Yes!', she thought, and plunged. She finned her way effortlessly through the wavy waterweed, now and then rising to the surface to snap up a fly. Her friends could hardly believe their eyes on their next visit to the swimming pool.

How old is Alicia this birthday? What do you think she felt about swimming? Do you know what a trout is? What is Alicia going to do? How do you think Alicia expects to change after swimming as a fish? What surprised her friends when they next went to the swimming pool? How do you know? What clues tell you so?

Reading Between the Lines Set Two

Story 9

'That's three magicians I've tried who can't manage the 6th of April', Mrs Gray said, putting away her phone in despair. 'We'll just have to settle for Mr Wonder.' The day of the party came and Mr Wonder arrived in a flurry of bags, wands and clothes, with a cage holding a rabbit, a pigeon and a tortoise. The children watched agog, as Mr. Wonder got everything ready and called for Zoe to come out and help him. 'For a ninth birthday I always do a special trick', he said. 'I'm going to make these animals disappear.' He covered the cage and gave it a tap with his wand. 'All say abracadabra with me', he told the children. When he lifted the cloth, the rabbit and the tortoise were still there, but instead of the pigeon there was a pile of feathers.

Was Mr Wonder a good magician? What date did Mrs Gray book the magician to come on? Who was having a party? How old was the birthday girl? Did Mr Wonder surprise everyone by doing a brilliant trick? How do you know? What clues tell you so?

Story 10

Adam was driving everyone mad with his new phone. 'If I have to see any more selfies of Adam standing in front of some statue, Adam going down the river on a boat or Adam watching a rugby match', his flatmate Jon said, 'so help me, I'll pinch his phone and drop it down a drain.' 'I can sort it out for you in a week', said a strange voice from the ceiling. 'Just say "Animalitis" and clap your hands three times.' Completely bewildered and feeling something of a fool, Jon nevertheless did as the voice told him. The next time Adam took a selfie, he was horrified to see that instead of his own face, a frog looked back at him from the screen. He erased the picture and tried again. This time, it was a rat and the next time, a squirrel with a very ugly look in its eye.

What had Adam been doing that annoyed everyone so much? What did the mysterious voice make happen? Do you think Adam was cured of taking and sending so many selfies? Do you think the magic went on working for ever? How do you know? What clues tell you so?

Part 2 - Stories

Adventure theme

Story 1

Jack, Lily and their cousin, Flo, were on holiday with Jack and Lily's Mum, Sal, and her partner, Finn. The holiday park was out in the country and the children wanted to go and explore. Jack managed to persuade the parents to let him, Lily and Flo go off exploring for a bit. They promised to be back by midday. On the far side of the site, away from the caravans, there was a lake, fringed by trees. In the middle of the lake, there was a wooded island. The children made their way towards the lake. 'Look!', exclaimed Flo. 'A boat!' Tied to a post, bobbing gently was a little wooden boat with two seats and two oars. They looked at each other. 'Shall we?', said Jack 'Hey', said Flo. 'This is a real adventure.' When they got there they pulled the boat up onto the mud and set off through the trees. Now the wind had got up and it looked like it was going to rain again. Jack looked at his watch. 'Guys, look, it's 11.30 now and we said we'd be back by twelve.' They retraced their steps to where they'd left the boat. 'But this is where we pulled it up onto the mud, wasn't it', said Lily, sounding anxious. Across the lake, they could see something blue, bobbing in and out of sight, in the distance.

When Jack said 'Shall we?' what was he talking about? Why isn't the boat where they had left it? What can they see on the lake in the distance? How do you know? What clues tell you so?

Story 2

Ravi tried to be friendly but the others just turned away from him. He was worried about going on the residential trip. The first night was awful. Declan and Jared they completely ignored him. The next day, they went pond dipping, which was brilliant and, in the afternoon, they visited a big old house full of lots of things from history. There was a lovely park around the house where they had a picnic lunch and then they were allowed to go and play for a bit. Down by the lake, was a little boathouse and Ravi followed the others to see what they could find. On the way, he saw swans gliding along the lake and deer on the hillside. This was magical to a boy who had never really visited the countryside. He forgot about the others as he watched the swans. By the time he reached the boathouse, he was surprised by a banging noise. He looked around, puzzled. As he got nearer, he saw Jared's face at the window. Jared, who was usually the boss of everything, was looking scared. Ravi thought for a moment, then he worked it out! Later that evening, Jared tapped Ravi on the shoulder. 'Thanks, mate, you were amazing!' After that, Ravi never felt left out again.

Where do you think Ravi lived? Why had he never seen swans before? What was the banging noise? Why did Jared look scared? What did Jared thank Ravi for? Why did Ravi not feel left out after that? How do you know? What clues tell you so?

Story 3

I love it out here, under the leaves or basking in the sun by the wall. But today was different. The air was sharp, the sun went down a bit early and it felt like the Earth tilted just a tiny fraction. So I knew it was time to make the journey from the safety of the garden into that great mass of stone and unknown. As I make my way from the warm, gentle earth towards the great grey stone thing, I wonder how on earth I am going to get through. She said I am supposed to get under something called the Door, then scuttle like mad for what will seem like ages. Then I will find a weird, complicated series of ascenders, interspersed with flat places. Somehow, I have to navigate this system. After what seems like a lifetime, the ascenders end. Now, just a flat, rough expanse. Silently, I cross this desert-like space until I reach the edge. The next bit seems to be made of wood, but smooth, not like the trees outside. There is a narrow space between two of these slices of wood, just big enough to squeeze into. I gather my legs around me and carefully clamber into this dark space. This feels better, dark and enclosed, a safe place for me to start spinning.

Who do you think 'she' might be? What kind of creature is the writer of this text? What time of year is it? What is the writer going to spin? How do you know? What clues tell you so?

Reading Between the Lines Set Two

Story 4

Magda shivered slightly as she looked around her. She had never been up here before. She couldn't hear the familiar sound of her Mum clattering about the kitchen, singing along with the radio. Once her eyes got used to the semi-darkness, she saw there was a small window at the far end and a large wooden table in the centre. The walls were lined with large, dusty boxes and a very old-looking teddy bear was propped against the table leg. It was then that she heard it. A slight scuffling sound, coming from the far end, by the window. Magda took a step forward and the sound stopped. She looked over her shoulder, back towards the door, making sure she'd left it open. Then she tiptoed very slowly towards the window. 'Scritch, scratch' – there it was again. It seemed to be coming from the box under the window sill. This box didn't have a lid like the others, so Magda crept forwards and peered in. At first, she couldn't see anything but then she made out two, no, three shapes huddled in the bottom of the box. Magda couldn't believe her eyes. She quickly crossed the room and went down the stairs two at a time to tell Mum. Maybe her wish would come true!

Where is Magda? Why does Magda shiver slightly? What do you think might be in the box? What is Magda going to tell her mum? What is Magda's wish? How do you know? What clues tell you so?

Story 5

Noah and his brother, Harrison, set off across the moor. It had snowed in the night and was still snowing lightly. Their aim was to reach Hadread's Tor. The guidebook said you could see the foundations of a Celtic village settlement just below the Tor. They walked for about an hour and then Harrison felt in his pocket and suddenly looked alarmed. 'Oh no!', he exclaimed. 'The map!' 'Oh, for goodness sake, Harry', said his brother. 'Well, it's not worth going back now we've got this far. Just as well there's snow on the ground. We can just follow our footprints back!' It was about midday when they arrived at the towering lump of rock. They found a sort of grid of stones about the size of a tennis court. 'This must be the village', said Harrison and they spent the next half hour wandering through what could have been paths and huts, imagining the lives of those ancient people. The snow had turned to rain so they decided to go back. 'All we've got to do is follow the footprints', pointed out Harrison. Then they looked at each other, puzzled. 'What are we going to do now?', asked Noah, staring at the expanse of grey ahead of them.

Why did Harrison look alarmed when he felt in his pocket? Why did Noah think it didn't matter? Why do they look at each other in a puzzled way? How do you know? How are they going to find a solution? What clues tell you so?

Reading Between the Lines Set Two

Story 6

Gareth felt as if he might die of excitement. To be the youngest person ever to do it! He had applied when he was still under 18, but the selection process had taken nearly a year. The final fitness checks had been carried out and the final briefing given. He had said a six-months' goodbye to his parents and seen them taken across the tarmac to the observation tower. Through the window, he could see the rocket in its final stage of preparation, with busy groups of technicians and scientists bustling about. Some of the crew were already walking in the direction of the beautiful sleek machine. Gareth took a deep breath. 'See you soon, Jupiter', he whispered to himself and moved to the door.

What is Gareth about to do? What is special about him? How old do you think he is? How long is he going for? What are they hoping to explore? How do you know? What clues tell you so?

Story 7

From the holiday house in Corfu, the coast of Albania was visible across the sea. At night, lights appeared among the trees there, where no villages existed, and not even a single house. A profitable trade in contraband was said to take place across that narrow stretch of sea. One evening, Leo was exploring an inlet along the coast when two burly men rose up from among the bushes and seized him. A grubby hand was clamped over his mouth and his own hands were fastened behind his back. Leo was in no doubt about what sort of people these were and that they were not friendly. There was no point in struggling: it was two to one and the men were a lot larger than Leo. He struggled to remember the few words of Greek he knew. His Albanian vocabulary amounted to zero.

What were the lights that appeared among the trees on the Albanian coast? What sort of people were there, and what were they doing? Who do you think grabbed Leo and tied his hands? Why is he trying to remember some Greek words? Does he speak any Albanian? How do you know? What clues tell you so?

Part 2 - Stories

Story 8

The track had dwindled to a narrow footpath, so Jeff and Mike had parked the van. Carrying the basic necessities and ropes and pitons on their backs, they had been walking up steep, stony tracks for over an hour. In that time, they hadn't seen a sign of human habitation. This was isolation even more extreme than the Alpine Club had promised. The sun was beginning to go down and the air was becoming bitingly cold. At last, they rounded a corner where the path hugged a stretch of vertical cliff and there in front of them was the hut. It did not look welcoming. The roof was short of several slates and two panes of glass in the single window were missing. The water tank had been knocked over. As Jeff stepped forward to unlock the door, he saw that the surface was scarred by deep scratches and huge paw prints led away into the forest.

What had these men come to do? What do you think they thought about the scratches on the door and the paw prints? Is there anyone to whom they can turn if they need help? Had the men been expecting to stay in a fairly isolated place? What makes you think so? How do you know? What clues tell you so?

Story 9

Finlay found himself clinging to the underside of the boat, salt water stinging his eyes and the cold beginning to penetrate through his wetsuit and lifejacket. The waves buffeted him, making it hard to keep his grip on the slippery wood. He could see Oliver clutching hold of the other side. Thank goodness they were both OK so far. The bad news was that the tide was going out, so they would be drifting further and further from the shore. Finlay thought back to how it had happened. Just one moment when he'd misjudged the wind and paid for it many times over. It was half an hour, during which Finlay began fear for their lives, before they heard the roar of an engine and saw the bow wave of a boat approaching, with the familiar letters RNLI visible through the spray.

What has happened to Finlay and Oliver? Are they on the sea or on a river, do you think? Would they become safer or in more danger the longer they were there? Are they going to be all right? How do you know? What clues tell you so?

Copyright material from Catherine Delamain & Jill Spring (2018),
Reading Between the Lines Set Two, Routledge

Story 10

The group had abseiled down, leaving behind the sun-warmed scents of wild thyme and heather for the dank of rocky walls, the dripping of water and increasing darkness. Lighted only by their torches, they moved forward, following Kenny deeper and deeper into the hillside. Every so often, he called back to check that they were all OK, his voice echoing eerily off the stony walls and roof. They could clearly see how the stone slabs on the floor had been cut by human hands and there were other signs that humans had once been here. At last, Kenny stopped to let them catch up. The torches lit the mirror-like surface of a sheet of water and beneath it lay the shapes of broken statues. This was what they had come to see.

What is the group doing? Is it summer or winter, do you think? Had this cave been discovered already? Did the group know what to expect when they reached the lake in the middle? How do you know? What clues tell you so?